TANS

TANS

The TANS Collection, Volume I

Edited by John Klawitter

Writer's Showcase
San Jose New York Lincoln Shanghai

TANS
The TANS Collection, Volume I

Writer's Showcase
an imprint of iUniverse, Inc.

For information address:
iUniverse, Inc.
5220 S. 16th St., Suite 200
Lincoln, NE 68512
www.iuniverse.com

ISBN: 0-595-21729-X

Printed in the United States of America

CONTENTS

FORWARD

*By now, you may have read **Body of Secrets**, James Bamford's best selling book on the U.S. history of electronic intelligence gathering. If you haven't, you might do well to pick up a copy, for it provides excellent background for understanding the dangers and nuances of the modern world of spying. Our group of stories, **The TANS Collection**, gathers personal memoirs and recollections from the same body of intelligence people Bamford sketches in his work. In **The TANS Collection** you'll find the experiences of real-life spooks and spies told in their own words. This isn't a fictional, made-up world, but rather the true tales of young Americans, often fresh out of high school and college, sent around the world on interesting, difficult and sometimes dangerous assignments vital to the National Security.*

*You may wonder how and why such a collection came to exist. The truth is, it was almost an accident. For several decades, a group of ex-intelligence people known as **The Old Spooks & Spies** has met to talk over their experiences and remember old times. **The Old Spooks & Spies** is made up of Americans and their allies, soldiers who generally served in military intelligence, that is, in the gathering of covert information from neutral or unfriendly forces. In getting together, the members of **The Old Spooks & Spies** often discussed a common problem—it wasn't so much the Top Secret nature of the things they had done for their country (much of which had been de-classified over the years), but rather that they felt the effects of an anti-military bias, a closed-minded unwillingness that their voices be heard. At least, that's the way it seemed to them, and from that common experience came a special comradeship that lead, slowly and hesitantly at first, to the telling of their stories.*

Some of them had found that, since the beginnings of our active involvement in Southeast Asia in the 1960s, people in positions to publish in this country did not consider the experiences and ideas of those who served in the military to be worthy of serious evaluation, much less publication, unless they were of an obvious anti-war vein, or taught lessons of one-world enlightenment or contained subtle or not-so-subtle anti-patriotic themes. Many in the literary establishment put out the vibe that those who served in Vietnam couldn't have anything worthy to say unless they recanted and repented of their involvement.

The reasons for this inclination were ideological and often deeply personal, and are well recorded. *The Old Spooks & Spies* had experienced the real world and had stories to tell—and yet found as a general experience that there was little or no interest in publishing them.

Still, a good story will always find an audience; *The Old Spooks & Spies* began to swap their experiences at reunions and share them via the Internet. Over time, this evolved into the annual short story writing contest they called "The TANS Competition." The rules to entering TANS are simple: the writer must have served in U.S. military intelligence (or of our Allies), and the recollection has to be true. The winners of this competition proudly receive "an ornate but worthless piece of paper."

As for the name itself, some say TANS may stand for the 1st four letters of Tan Son Nhut, the airbase in South Vietnam where many members of *The Old Spooks & Spies* were stationed in the 1960's and early 1970's. Others will insist TANS stands for the words, That ain't no s***, an enthusiastic reminder that truth can, indeed, be as interesting as fiction.

Funny, sad, tragic, unexpected and outrageous, these stories open a window into the lives and feelings of a group of military people who endured and experienced much to protect our American way of life in uncertain times. Many, but not all, of the tales are from Southeast Asia, simply because of the length and depth of our involvement in the Vietnam War. Others are from Stateside or from the farthest corners of the world. After all, as the old underground intelligence slogan warns, In God we trust; all others, we monitor.

These then are the stories of the TANS, a collection of not-so-simple remembrances from a group of people who followed their countries need in uncertain times and lived to tell about it.

-John Klawitter, Senior Editor

ACKNOWLEDGEMENTS

This publication is a collective effort of the Old Spooks & Spies, the sponsoring organization for the annual TANS Short Story Contest. For further information on the organization or the contest, visit www.oldspooksand-spies.org.

Dave Parks created the Front Cover Illustration a highly creative rendering of covert strings running through the jungle, demonstrating the mission of the U.S. Army Security Agency in Southeast Asia. Not only a brilliant design artist, Dave Parks has also contributed a variety of personal stories and recollections to this collection.

Grateful thanks to Lynn Jensen-Klawitter and Tes Safavi for line-by-line edit and proofreading.

Throughout recorded history, military intelligence has always been of enormous value, and many historical references remain in our culture. The word 'marathon' is an allusion to the famous bit of intelligence passed on by the Greek runner Pheidippides, who in 490 B.C. ran 26 miles from Marathon to Athens to carry the news of an enormous victory over the Persians.

And when forced to deliver bad news, we often say 'Don't shoot the messenger.' Shooting the messenger was probably a convenient solution to the concern that the poor fellow was in many cases also a spy.

Our nation's history is full of tales of spies and spying. The immortal last words of Nathan Hale, "I only regret that I have but one life to lose for my country," were spoken in 1776 before he was hanged as a spy by the British. Spies were thick as thieves on both sides of the Civil War, annoying both the Union and the Rebels, and World War I had its notorious Mata Hari, an exotic Dutch dancer who was executed by the French in 1917.

Here's a story from World War II, the straight-forward recollections of a man who was drafted into the war and learned to shoot both clear pictures and straight bullets.

WITH MY CAMERA AND MY CARBINE

By Norman G. Jensen

I left my new wife, went through basic training and was sent across the Atlantic to Europe on a troop ship. By then it was October of 1944 and the North Atlantic can be murder. It was rough weather all the way with the ship often covered with water. There was constant turning and tossing, and everybody was sick most of the time, all of us packed in that confined space and no going topside for even a gasp of fresh air for fear of being swept overboard. I was lucky; I always had a strong stomach and so I didn't get

1

sick, but it was almost as bad watching the other guys spill their guts without end, and the smell—well, you can imagine…

We landed in Marseilles and spent the next couple of months helping push the Germans out of France. I remember our unit, the American 70th Infantry, took the border town of Forebach, as can be seen in any military history of the war. But at this point we were told to pull back and let the French soldiers walk into the town with the bands playing and the newsmen snapping away. American soldiers had liberated the last major town in France with our own sweat and blood, but then we who had done all the work were told to pull back and let the French ride in style to parade around and take the glory, to show the world how great they were in the war. Believe me, the G.I.s didn't like that but it was politics and not anything you could do about it.

We had finally come to the western edge of France, but we didn't stop there. In a way, we were only getting started. We crossed the Rhine at Forebach and went through Saarbrucken on the other side. At least on the German side we found a mining firm that had showers and tubs and we all had our first bath in five months. Before that, while crossing France, the only way to keep your body clean was to fill a helmet with water and wipe yourself with soap and water. But now we were in Germany, and the Germans were giving up their own ground slowly and with a big grudge.

I was a photographer working in the G2 section attached to the 274th Infantry, 70th Army. My job was to take photographs of points of vital concern that the allies had bombed so our intelligence analysts could determine our effectiveness. It was important to know if bridges or high points such as church steeples or buildings needed further attention from our bombers or artillery. I had an assistant and my own jeep, and the jeep pulled a small trailer containing my photographic supplies and equipment.

We were always looking for places where enemy spotters or snipers could hide, and I felt good about my job. I knew our work was saving many G.I. lives, particularly as we were advancing across the *Vaterland* against such stubborn resistance.

We continued pushing east away from the Rhine and a little south, and a few weeks later we were in Stuttgart. One day—this was still in February—I left my jeep with a private who worked for me and I went for a walk along with some of the officers. I occasionally did that, as they would want to have a first-hand inspection of some new town or area that we'd just taken over.

I always carried my cameras and a carbine. I liked my carbine. It used the same ammo as the M-1 field rifle and yet it was much lighter. I could fire short bursts of five rounds each, and I had several of the longer clips that carried 45 rounds.

I'd earned my marksman medal from basic training, and so I felt fairly confident I could shoot straight. Still, I'm not trying to give you the idea I did this all the time. I wasn't an experienced infantryman, and I knew it. But in the army soldiers are expected to pick up a weapon and use it when necessary, no matter what their regular army job is.

I remember this particular day was bright, but cold. Stuttgart had been heavily bombed and as we walked down the center of the street there was the rubble of bombed-out buildings on either side.

It was strange. There would be places where civilians were waving and hanging out of the windows, trying to be friends, or at least not get shot. And in other areas it was very quiet, so quiet it made me nervous. The area wasn't yet secure, and from time to time we would hear shots ringing out in the near distance.

There were four of us. There was a Colonel and a Major in the center, I was on the left, and another enlisted man with a heavier M-1 rifle was on the right. The officers had pistols, which I personally didn't feel would be much good, excepting maybe at close range. As there was nothing of significance to photograph at that moment, I'd slung my cameras and was carrying my carbine on the ready.

All of a sudden, there was a rifle shot from nearby, and a bullet panged off a stone wall that was behind and to the side of us. I looked around and saw a German soldier trying to squirm away. Without thinking, my carbine came up. I gave him a burst and he fell over, arms flung out. He was wearing the German uniform and was certainly dead, so we hurried on past without stopping to look him over.

That's how the Germans would do it; they would leave soldiers hidden behind to pop up and snipe at us from close range as we advanced. You had no choice but to go on into it. We continued for maybe another half block and another shot slapped by; somebody else was shooting at us. I figured this was an even closer call as I heard the bullet whiz by my ear. I spotted this new shooter and again without thinking my carbine came up and I got him with my first burst. For the second time in just a few minutes, a German soldier fell over.

That was over 50 years ago, but I never forgot those moments. I was awarded the Bronze Star, and I have always been proud of that, but honestly, I felt even luckier just to be alive.

After that, we went on in pretty much the same way, pushing deeper and deeper into Germany until the war was finished. And when it was over, I returned home to my wife and started my career in the shipping industry as an importer/exporter. We had two little girls, and they grew up and gave me grandchildren.

I sometimes think, *What if I had been a little slower, or hadn't been able to shoot straight?* I guess that in that case I myself, the two officers and the other enlisted man might all be dead, and somewhere in Germany today maybe there would be two old men telling their grandchildren about the time they killed some American soldiers and lived to tell the tale. But that is the way of war. It doesn't ask if you are an accomplished infantryman or simply a cameraman-soldier, and it doesn't ask how you feel about shooting a fellow human being. It just wants to know you can shoot fast and straight. And if you can, maybe you will be lucky enough to live through that day and eventually get through the war.

The young men and women who end up in military intelligence are generally very quick-witted. They display an aptitude for machinery, for learning foreign languages and for adapting to unusual situations. They seem to be born with an impatience for pomp and foolishness, a quirky sense of humor and a general curiosity about and zest for life in general. Witness the early recollections of a young car thief who lied to the judge about his age, was given a choice of jail or military service and sent to Korea where he was seriously wounded by the enemy—before he reached the age of 17.

A MISSPENT YOUTH

Or
Don't Let The Sun Set On Your Ass In Newark, N.J.

By Jack Waer

We were living in a 3-story walk-up. Three apartments to a floor with one bathroom at the end of the hall that served for all three apartments on the floor. I remember we were on the 3rd floor front. I was 12 years old, going on 17. Street-wise, you know?

After school, I used to wander the streets seeking whatever opportunities would present themselves. I had good scams going. I'd wander down to the train station and steal hubcaps from the cars parked there. One from each car on the side that faced the station, so the owner would notice it was gone when he returned. At the exit, I would sit on the ground with 10 or so stolen hubcaps, just waiting for business to come along. As the owners drove out and saw the hubcaps matching theirs, I would sell them back for fifty cents apiece.

The train station scam was a limited opportunity as I figured I could only return once or twice a month before the owners would start to get wise. I was going to have to branch out to other areas. I came up with the idea of standing in an empty parking space in the center of Newark where parking was at a premium. When someone tried to park, I would stand there and not move, telling them I was saving the space for my mother, who was circling the block. (My mother didn't drive.) I could usually con fifty cents or so out of the frustrated driver.

One day, Salvatore Buono, a classmate, told me there was easier money to be had. His father owned Buono's Barber Shop and ran a bookie operation on the side. Soon I was running numbers as a bag boy and picking up $20 to $30 a week. This worked well until I got caught. I was sent to juvenile court and put on probation. Buono Senior gave me $100 for not squealing. My parents were pissed, so I ran away from home and hitch-hiked to Florida. I ended up in Miami Beach, working in a Jewish hotel. I was washing dishes and sleeping on the beach, and enjoying two free meals a day from the hotel. But my luck wouldn't hold.

A few months later I got caught in a sweep against child labor laws. I ended up in juvenile hall, where they found out I was a runaway. The Florida State Police took me to the Georgia state line, Georgia State Police to the South Carolina state line, and so on, all the way back to New Jersey. Oh Happy Days!! My parents, the police and the court were so impressed they sent me to the Annadale Boys Reformatory.

I spent my next two years at Annadale. While there, I skipped two grades in school and was classified as "Exceptional," testing in with an I.Q. of 145. Annadale was a very instructional experience; my fellow inmates taught me how to steal cars. I was released and sent back to Newark, where I spent my 15th year as a Junior in high school. I also took the opportunity to return to Buono's Barber Shop, where I explained my new talent to the proprietor. From then on, I went to work after school stealing cars for Buono. He would hand me a slip of paper with a year, model and color of car. The colors were difficult, but I would wander the streets of Newark, looking for example for a dark colored 1950 Buick 4 door sedan. If I was lucky, the keys would be in it. If not, I'd hot-wire it, drive through the Lincoln Tunnel, make the first left, the second right, and go to the building with four big sliding doors. I'd drive up to the third door and honk four short blasts. The door would slide up. I'd drive in, park, get out, accept $100, and go back to Newark.

It was an easy and profitable life, and I drifted into my Senior year of high school on a bit of a high. But it all came crashing down in January of 1952 when I was arrested for 32 counts of Grand Theft Auto. By my count, it had to be more, because I'd stashed away $5,300, not counting what I'd spent. My parents, the police and the court were not impressed with my free enterprise undertakings. I stood in front of the judge on February 4, 1952. I remember it well; it was my 16th birthday.

The judge said, "Waer. You are accused of 32 counts of Grand Theft Auto, and there is no doubt of your guilt."

"Uh huh," I replied.

"I have your juvenile record in front of me. You've been in trouble with the law since you were twelve years old."

"Uh huh," I said.

"You are incorrigible!"

"Uh...judge. What does incorrigible mean?"

"Shut up!"

"Uh huh," I said.

The judge's face assumed the grim look of one who must do his duty. "I have several choices, young man. You will either be sentenced to Trenton State Prison for 3 to 5 years, or you can enlist in the U.S. Army for 3 years. Either way, the sun will not set on your ass tonight in Newark, New Jersey."

"Uh huh."

"If you choose the army and are honorably discharged after three years, I will personally see to it that your records with this court are destroyed. On the other hand, if you choose prison, I will personally guarantee you that I will hound you for the rest of your life! Now, young man, what is your choice?"

"Navy?" I asked.

"Army!" he thundered.

"Okay. Army."

So they escorted me to the Newark Induction Center, where I flunked the physical. I was five foot nine inches, and weighed only 104 pounds. That was two pounds under the minimum weight for my height. So the cop who escorted me took me to the local A&P Market where he bought me five pounds of bananas. He made me eat them all, and by the time he escorted me back to the center, I weighed in at 106.5 pounds. As the sun was setting in Newark, I was on a bus headed for Fort Dix. I was in the U.S. Army.

I found it easier than reform school. At the Fort Dix Reception Center, corporals and sergeants were trying to make it hard on us nugs. For three days they gave us batteries of tests, short haircuts and our army fatigues. On the 4th day, a young captain was questioning why I had not graduated from high school. I explained that I was a Senior, and had been due to graduate in June, but the court had come up with another idea.

I was told to come back the next day to see him. When I did, he had a staff sergeant bring me to clothing stores. I was issued three sets of sun tans and two sets of Ike jacket uniforms, a sun tan piss cutter, an OD piss cutter and brown shoes. I was shown how to wear brass, and escorted back to the captain. He had a set of orders assigning me to Company A, 113th Tank Battalion, 50th Armored Division of the New Jersey National Guard. And my assignment? To finish High School! Oh, shit! I was back in Newark again.

But in the army you don't ask why, you just do it. I went back to Newark and reported in to Company A. They had an active duty 1st sergeant there. I lived in the armory and went to school. I did my homework after school, ate supper and cleaned the armory as my daily routine. I spent weekends polishing tanks, and on drill nights I learned how to drive a tank. I had to go to school in uniform, and since the Korean War was going on, I got more ass in 4 months than I'd ever had in all my years in school. I had no contact with my former associates in crime, though I found myself looking fondly on unattended cars from time to time.

The day after my graduation I was back at Fort Dix with orders in hand. I thought I was going to be sent to Basic Training as a Private E-2 instead of an E-1. But, as you know, FUBAR reigns in the military. They thought I was coming back from leave after Basic. I was sent to a replacement depot and put on a troop train to Oakland, California. There I was issued a BAR and loaded on the USS Edwin D. Patrick. Thirty-two days later I landed at Inchon, Korea. I was scared shitless. Nobody seemed to care. I was assigned to a unit and found myself in Kaesong, which was actually above the Demilitarized Zone, somewhere in North Korea.

My first evening, I was assigned to a squad that had to go out on patrol. We came over a hill and I saw more Orientals with weapons than I ever hope to see again! Perhaps it was probably only a couple of squads, but to me it seemed like hundreds!

I didn't have time to think about it, because they swarmed us and we were engaged in hand-to-hand combat. I lost 16 teeth from a horizontal butt stroke and we were cutting a chogi for our own lines. Back at the unit, when I sat down, it felt kind-of squishy and wet. I thought I had shit in my pants. I was scared and embarrassed. A corporal yelled "Medic!", and I wondered who had been shot. It turned out to be me!

I had a long open wound across the right lower cheek of my ass. I was sent back to Inchon where a medic changed the dressing on my ass and tried to pull the remaining roots of my teeth with no pain killer. He was using a pair of pliers from a jeep toolbox. This did not impress me, so I told him I'd wait a while. I was finally sent back to my old troop ship, the USS Edwin D. Patrick. There they gave me 47 stitches in my ass, and knocked me out while they repaired the damage to my mouth. I was told I was being sent back to the states. My entire Korean War experience has lasted 17 and a half hours.

On the 31 day trip back to the States, one highly agitated major approached me. He told me I couldn't be in the army until I was 17 years old, and couldn't be in a combat zone until I was 18. He told me that, upon reaching Oakland, I would be hospitalized until fully recovered. Then I would be discharged and sent back to Newark. I told him I couldn't have that. I poured out my sad story of the judge, and no basic training. The major actually broke down and cried. He cursed the army and the court system, and said he would see what he could do. Several days later he came back with a deal. The army would hide me out until I was 17, but I had to go to Basic first. Then, because of my high scores, I could go to an army language school. Remembering the judge's admonition, I quickly accepted.

When we arrived at Oakland, I was sent to Letterman Army Hospital. After I mended, I was sent to Fort Ord as a PFC. I had a Purple Heart, a Korean ribbon, and a National Defense ribbon. When my 1st sergeant at Ord heard what had happened, he went ballistic. He made me the company runner for my 8 week's stay, and to this day I've never had basic training. After that, I was sent across the bay to the Monterey Language School for a three month course in Indo-Chinese.

When I graduated, I volunteered for Airborne at Fort Bragg. Three weeks later, I volunteered for Ranger School in Panama. Four months later, I was in the Philippines for jungle training. And in November of 1953, I jumped into Dien Bien Phu with a 10 man Ranger team. I spent 6 months at Beatrice, leaving there on April 27, 1954. I was sent to the PI and then back to Bragg.

On February 3, 1955, I was honorably discharged from the U.S. Army. I returned to Newark one day shy of my 19th birthday. I had two rows of ribbons, including 2 Purple Hearts. I was sitting in the 3rd floor front apartment, looking out of the window and drinking a beer when there was a knock at the door. It was a cop accompanied by my old probation officer. They took me to see the judge. I showed my honorable discharge. I was still in uniform, and the medals gleamed on my chest. The judge congratulated me for turning my life around. He took me into his chambers, took out my records, and burned them in a metal trash can.

"Corporal Waer," he said, "You have fulfilled your part of the bargain. And I have fulfilled mine. Now, don't let the sun set on your ass in Newark, New Jersey, this evening. Get out of my sight!"

I was escorted to the recruiting station, where I reenlisted for six years. I was off to Monterey, to study Chinese at the Army Language School. And to this day, never again has the sun set on my ass in Newark, New Jersey.

No matter where they go, the gatherers of covert intelligence have a tendency to pick up pets. They like monkeys and parrots as well as dogs and cats. Never mind that they have learned to read code coming in over static-laden headsets at blinding speed or can fix electronic equipment with stunning ingenuity; these are young men and women who came from your city, your town, your neck of the woods. On the other hand, situations could develop…what do you do when bitten by the ocelot you brought home from the market vendor, or when you wake to find your pet boa wrapped affectionately around your leg like a steel cable?

In the decades after the shooting war stopped in Korea it was necessary to maintain an intense listening operation in South Korea because of the massive unfriendly North Korean presence just north of the demilitarized zone. Korea in the 1960s wasn't at all like the U.S., where dogs are given rabies and distemper shots on a regular basis. But that didn't seem to matter. There were stray dogs and lonely soldiers in a far place who needed a hint of their old life back home.

TAGI'S END

By Mac Maguire

It's funny, the things that happen in the army, the moments that maybe don't mean anything, but you remember them clear as a bell even after all the years in between. Here's a crazy moment I'll never forget. It was summer in 1964. I was in Korea, stationed with B Company of the 508th ASA Group. Our ASA compound was perched right above the water plant in a corner of Camp Casey. Camp Casey was the headquarters of the 7th Infantry Division. It was located about 35 miles north of Seoul, just off Military Service Road #1, in the small town of Tongduchon.

The compound was somewhat isolated and we had guard towers all around. It was completely cut off from Camp Casey proper, and even the division MPs weren't allowed access. We hired Korean guards under contract to guard our compound, but we didn't trust them. The word was, they were low-level agents for the *Chung Bo Bi Da*, the Korean equivalent of the CIA, detailed to us in the hope that we'd slip and let something out. They were all veterans of the South Korean Army, and tended to be twitchy on the trigger finger, and they could be very hard-core. I saw one of them shoot out the front tires of the Division Commander's sedan when he failed to halt at the gate.

Our secrecy and our security measures made the compound a self-sufficient little community. We were not officially allowed civilian clothes at all, but we routinely wore them in our compound. We even had our own club, the Tiki Club. I guess you could say we had our own style; even down to the pack of semi-wild dogs we allowed the run of the compound. There was Pete, the puppy machine. There was Scuz, who chased trucks until he caught one, bit the tire, and was snuffed. And the popular Tagi, the little almost-sort-of-basset hound. Tagi grew to be quite fat, which is how he got his name; Tagi is Korean for pig.

The dogs may have been our companions, but they were also a great backup security system, and accomplished ratters. They hated anyone they didn't know. They would bark at and chase any stranger who dared hit what they considered their turf. If you know the official army way, you realize how easily a pack of unruly dogs could present big problems in the wrong situation. But we usually rounded them up and locked them in the motor pool when we heard official company was coming.

Our Company Commander, Captain John Tracy, and 1st Sergeant Scagliotti were pretty understanding, but they drew the line at letting the dogs sleep in the barracks. And they wouldn't allow them to be fed from the tables in the mess hall. As the mess hall rules were pretty hard to enforce, Mess Sergeant "Pops" Hellickson spent a lot of his time giving our four-legged friends the boot. They were naturally attracted to the mess hall as the cooks put out the leftovers for them.

Korean winters were freezing cold, but the summers were beastly hot. In the winters the fierce wind would blow a talcum powder like fine dust into everything, making it hard on the equipment. But in the summers we had the monsoon season, and you know what moisture can do to electronics.

I remember one sweltering summer afternoon I was having trouble with a 1.5k generator that refused to work when I heard yelling in the distance, half way across the compound. I remember being distracted and dropping a wrench I'd been using. I wiped my sweaty brow and looked out and there was Tagi, running around the compound like he'd gone mad. He was foaming at the mouth and bouncing off everything in his path. I narrowed it down right away; either Tagi'd gotten into some lemon meringue pies or he'd gone hydrophobic. Since Pop hadn't been known for his lemon meringue, I figured Tagi for one diseased canine. Troops scattered everywhere. Charley Ridgeway, the crypto repairman even tried to climb the fence around the operations building. Anything to get out of the way of the mad dog.

Fred Pruden went into action immediately. Fred was working in the COMSEC office in the operations building when he sized up what was going on. He ran down the hall, grabbed a riot gun off the hooks in the CQ office and headed for the lower compound. What he found when he got there was a scene from the Keystone Kops. There were cooks, G.I.s and Korean houseboys running every which way and climbing anything they could find, while the mad Tagi dashed first this way and then that.

Fred herded Tagi into the lower barracks by firing a couple rounds in the air. He ordered all of us away and entered the building alone. Later, he told us that he found the dog cowering in the latrine. It was a four or five-hole shitter, complete with stalls with hinged doors. Tagi was huddled in the last stall. Fred tried to talk him out, but Tagi was intimidated by the blasts from the riot gun. He wasn't coming out.

Fred felt he had no other choice; he carefully advanced on the stall, gingerly opened the door, and fired. His only problem was that he was in a concrete building and that riot gun was loaded with double-ought buck high-brass magnums. The blast from his shotgun put Tagi down, but it also blew up the commode and most of the stall as well.

After a time, the medics arrived. They determined Fred had to be treated for shrapnel wounds from the exploding porcelain throne. But that wasn't the end of his bad luck. The medics sent what was left of Tagi to Japan for tests, and it turned out the poor dog did have rabies. So Fred had to undergo a series of very painful shots.

And Fred...well, that wasn't the last of his bad luck. I heard he died some few years later of wounds he received in Vietnam. It's so clear in my mind, it's hard to believe that happened over 35 years ago...I remember Tagi foaming around and Fred grimly going after him, just like it happened yesterday.

Over the decades since WWII, the Army Security Agency, or ASA for short, has set up listening outposts and stations at strategic locations around the world. Unfortunately, the most useful places are often difficult and remote, with climates that range from bad to horrible. A rocky island in the Aleutians that measures a mile from end to end, where the winds blow the almost constant icy rain and sleet in sheets parallel to the ground and the fishing is great if you can stand the cold. Arid mountains in Ethiopia and Turkey. Lonely lumps of rock a few thousand feet above the rice paddies of the Vietnamese delta. But it isn't always that way. Sometimes the troopers get lucky and are assigned to places where the weather is fine and the people are interesting—and sometimes very friendly.

SGT OLSEN GOES FISHING

By Harold E. Castle

This happened to me on Oki in 1968. On Okinawa, on the road that runs west past the old ASA Field Station Torii, and past Sobe and Yomitan, is a place the Americans named Bolo Point. It is about midway up the island on the China Sea side.

It was named Bolo Point because that was where the U.S. Army held an annual Pacific Region-wide Air Defense contest. During the contest, the Zoomie Service (U.S. Air Force) would launch a target drone and an ADA battery would get one chance to destroy it. They either got the drone or they *boloed*.

The topography of the point and the surrounding area is as varied as only a volcanic seamount island, with coral overlays, can be. To the west, the point drops a couple of hundred feet down a sheer coral cliff, the base of which is undercut in a concave curve of twenty-five to fifty feet. The waves there roll in from a deep underwater trough that fans out in roughly a western direction into the East China Sea.

To the south and southeast, Bolo Point slopes off from a fairly wide tabletop down to the water's edge. The surface all the way down is weathered lava, and there are places where water pools during storms. It creates natural saltpans, and traps sand where small plants and critters live.

To the north and northeast, the Point also has a pretty steep cliff, but since it is sheltered, it has some vegetation, small trees, brush and grasses. It is the home of the Habu, the only poisonous land snake in the Ryukyu Islands. Over the centuries, the Okinawans had dug and worn a fairly easy trail and steps in the lava. That is the easiest way to get down to the water. There is a narrow beach at the north side of the point that runs back slightly northeast, and then north. It gets wider and there is a pretty good area of water that goes to 40 or 50 feet deep from the shore out to the deep trench in front of Bolo Point.

Now at that time I was interested in free diving. One of my mentors, and a great dive buddy was SSG Steve "Sugar Bear" Woods. Steve fit the nickname well; he was short, stocky and strong as a bear. In the modern look-pretty army, Steve would have been in trouble because of his height/weight ratio, but he was in amazing shape. He could free dive in 60 to 60 feet of water with a bottom time of over 3.5 minutes. Sometimes he would even stay down 4 minutes.

Over the years, Steve, Tommy O. Mansfield, and some other ASA folks on Okinawa had developed some excellent free diving techniques and tools. One of these was a large nylon net bag holding a one-meter brightly colored beach ball. Another was to post a large diving flag on a stick on the beach wherever we were diving. When we arrived at an area where we wanted to dive, we would tie the dive flag to a tree limb or bamboo stick and jam it in the sand. Then we would wade out into the water carrying our gear and inflating the beach ball. By the time we had swum out to water deep enough to dive, the ball would be full and we would be pre-hyperventilated. We would tie about 100 to 125 feet of braided nylon rope to the net bag, and tie the other end to the handle of our spear gun, or snap it onto the belt loop in the back of our cut-off fatigues. Steve preferred tying to the handle, while I preferred the belt loop while swimming. Then I would snap-link it to the gun when I was ready to start hunting for fish. I also had the rope running through a snap link with a large loop of rope attached that I could hang on to.

The beach ball-and-net combination would support a lot of weight or pull, and we attached a waterproof bag to it. In there we would keep a pack of smokes, a lighter, and a couple of flares in case we found ourselves in trouble after dark. We also put in something for energy, and something potable that we could stomach at ambient temperatures. This last was to take the taste of rubber and saltwater out of our mouths. We found that cheap brandy or cognac worked well for this purpose, and those became my potables of choice.

If you have ever dove in the Pacific over lava and coral, you know that there are some weird and wonderful shapes and twists under the surface. The area off Bolo Point had all this, and great fishing, too. It was one of our favorite places to dive. We could get lobster, grouper and amberjack, and that made for all sorts of good eating. Steve once shot a 350-pound amberjack, but didn't kill it right away. He rode that beach bag for about four hours before the fish tired enough for him to dive down and put it away with a bang stick.

On one dive, I was hunting for grouper over what looked like a slit in the lava. We had explored this place a few days before and found that it was a hole in the lava where hot gas had been trapped back when it first had been formed. We had seen grouper swimming in there, so my intent was to lay on top of the slit for as long as possible. Then, if a grouper swam under, I would shoot it with my three ban gun, using a spear with a flint tip that, once impeded in the fish, opened out with two wings.

As I waited, I saw movement toward the oceanside opening of the hole. I started swimming towards the movement, gun aimed down. As I arrived at the top of the hole, the fish started to come out. I began taking up slack on the trigger. Then I saw the fish's nose. *Shark!* I thought. That would be good. But then, there was more nose and more shark until the eyes came out and I'm thinking *BIG SHARK!!* It was a good thing I didn't shoot, because when he came fully out, there was about 15 feet of great white shark swimming a bare 20 feet below me. Ever seen a person snorkel backwards? It can be done, trust me.

I did a triple tap with the butt of my knife on the handle of the gun, my signal to get Steve's attention. We headed up and met at the surface. We went ashore because, in that area, if there was one white shark, there probably were more, and we didn't want any fish blood attracting them to us. We made our way along the beach to the steps and climbed the cliff. I took my car back to Torii and went over to the NCO club for a little cool mouth refreshment in the form of "Heineys."

SFC "Ole" Olson was there, and Steve told him what I had seen. To Ole, 15 feet wasn't much, but it piqued his interest.

"See ya guys around," he said. With that, he left the club. I didn't think much of it at the time, though the barkeep commented it was kind of early for Ole to be gone after only about 8 or 10 beers. Steve and I passed the time trying to make up for Ole's lapse.

The next morning, we decided to try the area again. When we got there, we saw Ole's old 1958 Buick. Ole'd beat us there. And something was very odd about his car; he'd jacked up the rear end off both tires, and one of the weirdest contraptions I'd ever seen was bolted to one of the rear wheels. It looked like a 20-inch empty rim, and it was very deeply inset in the center, with a heavy steel hook welded into the bottom, with the open part of the hook facing toward the front of the Buick. There was a big roll of two inch braided nylon rope hooked in it, and a big coil of rope was strung out behind the car, running toward the cliff edge. There the rope ran through a double wooden bollard that was bolted to a cement pad.

As if that wasn't enough, the front end of the car was chocked with about a half dozen ten-by-twelve wooden beams. There were chains over the front axle and they were bolted to the beams. Steve said they were all bolted together, and then bolted down into some threaded receptacles used for hold-ing down something they used during the ADA competitions.

"Ever seen Ole fish for shark?" Steve asked me.

"Not to my recollection. Hell, I thought all Ole did was hold down the right corner barstool at the club.

Steve looked around and moseyed to the cliff edge. We looked out to the west and there was Ole, in a little boat. He was paddling as hard as he could into the afternoon sun. After a while he must have found the place he wanted, because he stopped and pulled a live chicken out of a bag. He impaled the chicken on two hooks of the biggest treble hook I'd ever seen. He took out another chicken and stuck it on the single hook. Even from where we watched, it looked like a mess, with chickens flopping and squawking and bleeding all over the place.

But Ole wasn't phased. He chunked the chickens in the water and started rowing as hard as he could toward the south end of the point. To me it looked like he was almost planing that old Okinawan rowboat. Fear or joy—or maybe both—can make a man come to an effort like that.

The rope gave a couple of jerks before Ole got back. A bunch of Okinawan fishermen had joined the party and were cheering him on. Ole increased his rowing pace, which didn't seem possible. You would have thought he was trying out for the shell singles at the Olympics.

He made landfall. One of the fishermen grabbed his boat and dragged it on shore, and at that moment the rope on the cliff started unwinding.

"Come on, Ole!" Steve yelled encouragement and waved a bottle of Heiney in his direction. "It's a good 'un, it's a good 'un!"

Ole got in our car. His face was beet red and he was out of breath. He swigged down his beer in one mighty gulp. Then he grabbed the one I'd just opened and swigged that one down, too. As he finished, Steve handed him a fresh one and he started in on that. He looked at the unwinding rope.

"He's bit, but he ain't hooked and set, yet!" Ole observed. He ran to the driver's side and started his car with the transmission in neutral.

"Hey, Castle!" he yelled at me, "soon as it's taut, yell at me! Soon as it's taut!" He pushed down on the clutch and put the car in gear.

I watched the rope run on and on.

"How much line you got here, Sergeant Olsen?" I asked.

"About three-quarter mile, I reckon. And when we're fishin', it's Ole, Nug. Gimme a beer." I gave him a beer and continued to watch the rope run.

"Next to last loop, Ole."

Just as I got the words out of my mouth, Ole slammed the transmission into high, revved the engine and popped the clutch. He immediately jammed it into low, popped the clutch a second time and gunned it again.

"He's hooked and set now, boys," Ole said with all the confidence in the world. "Let's go watch the show."

We all ran to the edge of the cliff and watched where the rope went into the water. It was moving sideways toward the southwest and literally slicking the water. There was a rooster tail from the rope that shot twenty or thirty feet in the air. Suddenly the rope started humming louder as the shark turned away from us and headed back to the west. The rope was going down.

"He's headed for the bottom. He's gonna try to cut it, I reckon." Ole started toward his old Buick. "I'll try to turn his head."

Ole got in the car and put it in second. He started feeding a little gas to his engine. Then he fed it a little harder, and then harder still. Finally, he got the shark's head turned. Now the rope was on the surface and heading straight toward us. We could see the dorsal fin and the tail fin. The tail looked like it was sticking about four feet out of the water. Of course, by that time I had several 16-ounce Schmidt's of Philadelphia in me, so it could have been four inches.

Steve helped Ole hand-line the rope as fast as they could, trying to bring in the slack and catch up with the shark. Then Ole grabbed the line and started yanking as hard as he could. This made the shark turn back out to the west. He took off at high speed again. This time, when he got to the end of the rope, he started tail walking as he tried to throw off the hook. It was like watching a billfish on one of those deep-sea fishing shows you see on television. I thought it was an awesome sight, even from over a half-mile away.

The fight the shark put up with Ole and his Buick went on for what seemed like an eternity, though it probably was just a couple of hours. Finally, the Okinawan fishermen came to a pidgin agreement with Ole, the general consensus being that the shark was getting tired. There were several puffs of smoke from some of the pits in the lava. They were getting fires ready for a grand cookout. One of the fishermen took off on his bicycle, heading for Sobe Village to alert the villagers, and another came up to the car with a couple of combat jugs of sake.

Ole took a couple of tugs on the rope and got in the Buick. He started up the engine and began reeling in the fish. He got it about half way to the cliff when it decided it still had some fight. Ole's old car bucked and heaved, the motor strained, and there was a smell of burning clutch in the air. Ole dropped it into neutral and let the shark run. The big fish tried to do the tail walk again, but now he couldn't get it out of the water. Once more, Ole began to reel the fish in, but now Ole himself was weaving as he waved the half-empty sake bottle around like a regal scepter.

This time the fish came in without further struggle. Ole had me standing on the edge of the cliff as his scout. Teetering was more like it, as I'd had quite a bit to drink myself. My job was to tell him when the fish was about 100 to 150 feet from the cliff. When it got that close, the Okinawans grabbed the rope. Ole put the Buick in reverse and they started walking the rope down the south side of Bolo Point toward the water line.

Meanwhile, one of the natives brought a three-wheeled truck with a couple of large wooden slabs. More people started to arrive on foot, on bikes, on mopeds. All of them were carrying something to eat and drink. There was a great deal of sake, akadama wine, and Orion Beer. This was going to be a fine beach party!

They got the shark landed, and it was in fact a great white. I seem to remember it was 19 feet long, but by that time I wasn't paying much attention, as I was distracted by a really good-looking young Okinawan lady. She was looking at me over her fan, and smiling. I mean, I like fishing and stuff like that, but this had the promise of true love. I felt she needed her cup refilled, and I was the only one with cold beer. Chivalry wins out every time.

The Okinawans butchered the shark, cutting great slabs of meat off and packing it away as fast as possible. When they got to what Ole called 'the good parts', he had them cut the flesh into two-inch steaks weighing a pound or more each. He divided this 'shark loin' up with everyone who had helped, and they got busy grilling the meat. They had already cooked fresh rice, steamed seaweed and other tasty dishes over the charcoal fires in the lava pits. Steve told me the same fire pits were used as signal fires for the men who fished by night. Very resourceful people, the Okinawans.

Some of the women, including Sumika (by now I'd found out her name), brought us our food, fed us, and plied us with drink. Others brought out musical instruments and started playing and dancing. The moon came out. Someone was dispatched to the club with Ole in tow, and they returned with more *'Melican Beeru and Wisky'*.

And then there was another cup of beer to be drunk and Sumiko's hand was on my arm, examining the hairs that had been bleached by the sun and sea. And there was a cup of sake, and the band played on.

The next morning I woke up in a fisherman's house in Sobe. I felt like I'd been playing leapfrog all night, but I really couldn't remember. There was a gentle knock at the door and a small hand swept the paper door aside. A smile, a pot of strong green tea, a few rice balls with green dried seaweed.

"You need-a seaweed today, berry berry strong for you 'cause you berry berry strong last night," Sumika said. A peek of white cleavage, a flash of white leg. A quick scrub of the teeth with the dregs in the cup by the bedside, and a grasp on a slender arm.

"No," she insisted, "Eat rice, eat seaweed, drink-a tea. Then I give bath. Then we see if seaweed strong as mamasan say." It wasn't, but it wasn't all that bad, either.

A couple days later, I ran across Ole in the club.

"Hey, Sergeant Olsen," I asked, "When we going fishing again?"

Probably one of the more complicated procedures we all have to suffer through is paying taxes. Civilians may not think much about it, but people in army intelligence pay taxes, too, just like everybody else. And when you factor in the standard bewildering military regulations and the reality that U.S. Army, Navy and Air Force intelligence-gatherers are assigned and re-assigned anywhere in the world, the results can stagger the imagination.

MY EXTRA BONUS

By R.W. "Butch" Williamson

In February of 1966 I reenlisted for 6 years. That was at Homestead Air Force Base in Florida, the one that got blown away by Hurricane Andrew a couple of years ago. When I re-upped, I had what they call a "maximum multiplier", that is, five times the normal re-up bonus. (Even though we were supposedly limited to a grand total of $2,000 in bonuses for our entire career.) With that 5X multiplier, my total bonus came to just over $7,000. I received an initial bonus of over a thousand dollars, minus 20% income tax. Every year after that, for the next five years, I was to receive another payment of almost a thousand dollars on the anniversary of my reenlistment. As I was sent to Vietnam, I not only received Hazardous Duty Pay ($65 a month), but also all the money paid in Vietnam was tax-free. It's important to remember this.

At the time, my 1st wife wrote me a Dear John letter. I went home to try and work it out with her, but to no avail. This was going to be a costly divorce, so I went into a self-preservation mode. I asked for and received the remaining five payments of my 5X multiplier bonus in one chunk sum. So this was almost five thousand dollars that my ex-wife wouldn't be able to make any claims against.

I did my first year in Nam, and then in August of 1967 was sent to our field station at Hakata, Japan. At the tax filing time for that year, I wrote the IRS and asked if the funds I'd received in Japan were taxable. The IRS replied that "all monies paid in Vietnam are tax-free." After I showed the army the letter I'd gotten from the IRS, they refunded nearly a thousand dollars that they'd taken out in taxes. Unfortunately, I lost the copy of the IRS letter as the Army finance folks kept all the materials relating to my pay records.

I say *unfortunately* because I then went through my tours in Hakata, back to Vietnam for a year and a half, to Vint Hill Farms Station outside of Washington D.C., two and a half years in our Torii Field Station at Sobe, Okinawa, and about half of my tour at the Field Station at Udorn, Thailand. By now it was 1976, a full eight or nine years after the army refunded my taxes. I was nearly half way through my next enlistment! Anyway, we had some smart-assed finance sergeant at Udorn that evidently had too much time on his hands, and he pulled my pay for two months! As I'd forgotten the exact amount of the refund ($956.40), I couldn't figure out why they were pulling that money from my pay. I went in to see the First Sergeant, and then the Sergeant Major. Our 1st SGT in Udorn just washed his hands and said there was nothing to be done. He couldn't give me any explanation of why my pay had been withheld. The guys in finance wouldn't even talk to me. Only the Sergeant Major was able to get me an explanation. It was because I'd apparently been paid an overage back in 1968 (for the 1967 tax year). And now, seeing as the army was moving pay operations to Ft. Ben Harrison in Indianapolis, they were doing away with local paperwork. And so they had done an audit on me and found what they'd found.

With that, it began to come back to me. I told them the whole story, just about like I'm telling you now, and the finance sergeant just farted me off. But I wasn't about to give up. I re-wrote the IRS and they went back to their files and came up with one of those old, barely legible copies of the correspondence we'd had years before. So I gathered up the SGM and went back in to the finance people. They weren't going to give me the time of day except that the SGM started making calls. Within a week, I had a check for $956.40. Great, right? Wrong. Remember, that was about two months of my take home pay. So they doubled me up one month and cut me off the next. I think there was something spiteful about those finance guys. I never heard a word of apology out of them, but I guess they must not have liked Udorn because, for some reason both of them had to leave early, and in a hurry.

Every once in a while in this lifetime, you get the break instead of being broken. And that's how I received my bonus twice, sort-of…

If you were already in the army and you were sent to Vietnam, you didn't have the same set of problems you might have had if you were a college kid or a liberal-minded professor and you got some papers saying to report for duty. Soldiers from all walks of life and all corners of the country had to come to grips with the bare facts of survival. There was no question they were going to Vietnam. The problem for them would be how to survive the experience.

Signing On For The Job

By Tom Kemper

The situation of the working man has always been a part of my life from my very early days. I spent many of my teenage years working farm and signing on for the harvest in the Kingfisher, Okarche and Piedmont areas of Oklahoma. And there, once you give your word, that work becomes your responsibility. I once got too close to the bottom strand of a barbed wire fence with my six-gang plow, and ping-ping-pinged about 100 yards of fence. After church on Sunday, I got to restring that fence, not with one of those high-tech fence-stretchers, but with a mouth full of staples and two claw hammers.

I grew up and found myself in the army, in Vietnam. We got to Phu Bai, which was a few kliks south of the DMZ, though why the Army Security Agency would send five Chinese linguists to Vietnam was—and still is—classified. Be that as it may, we were flown up from Saigon in a C-123. We were wearing Signal Corps brass, another deception, and we landed at the Hue/Phu Bai International Airport. It was a 5,000 foot concrete strip, surrounded by scrubby bushes and sand dunes. Some guy told us to grab our gear and get in the truck . We asked where we were going.

"Over there," he sighed, pointing across Highway One to the Phu Bai Compound.

Once we got there, we heard the rumor that it was an old French artillery base, but that wasn't true, or if it was, the French presence was long gone. For one thing, the buildings, painted puppy-shit yellow, had only been there a few years. The compound was an oval of about 80 acres, with a single-strand barbed wire fence around it. When I got there in 1964 they were building a new Ops building, and it was rumored they were spending about $2 million on it.

We racked out in some wood framed tents and contemplated our futures. We had some sandbagged M-60 bunkers, and a mortar pit with several 81 mm mortars and one 4.5 incher. We had HE rounds for them, but the pit's primary purpose was to fire illumination rounds out into the boonies, mostly for the benefit of the Direction Finding guys who were stuck over in the dunes by the airport—outside the wire. They had standing orders that they could ask for illumination any time they wanted, and they wanted it all night. I can't say I blamed them.

Our security was handled by a platoon from the 39th ARVN Ranger Battalion, whose home unit was fighting in the Delta. This was considered Rest & Recreation by those guys, because they could bring their families. They lived in a camp outside the wire. These little guys would go out at night on two-man patrols. Their mission was to kill people, presumably Viet Cong, and to bring back prisoners.

Although we had already been taken out in the boonies by those ASA Special Forces guys to familiarize ourselves with M-14s, M-60s and M-79s, it was decided that, due to the fact that we had only been there a few weeks, we were not to be trusted in combat. So we were assigned to the destruct crew. That meant that the security of the new Ops building was to be handled by us *Top Secret Crypto Dudes*. At that time, we had a 5-stage alert system, and we were always at 4. If there was hostile action going on nearby, we would go up to 3. When it heated up to 2, we were to open the CONEX where all the thermite was stored. We were to arm the thermite flat-file destroyers that, when ignited, would burn at 4500 F. That's hot enough to burn through steel and even the floor well into the ground. If we ever arrived at Stage 1, we were to scrape all the paper from desktops into a pile on the floor, dump gasoline on the pile and throw a thermite grenade on it.

We were members of the Destruct Crew and Lieutenant Ted Dahms gave our first briefing.

Ted was an ROTC out of Kansas University. He had jug ears and no body fat, to speak of. He'd had a good career in college running any distance longer than a mile.

He explained our defense position, "When the siren goes off, you are to report with your basic load. If the enemy has significantly penetrated the compound to where the OPs building is in danger, you are to assist in melting, burning and generally blowing the place up."

One of the guys raised a hesitant hand. "Uhh, Lieutenant, what do we do then?"

"You go and join the defense of the compound."

I raised my hand. "Lieutenant...? If the enemy's inside the compound and we've already blown the OPs, there's not gonna be a whole lot to defend, is there?"

He gave me a flat Midwestern stare. "Well, you hired out to work, didn't you?"

Some of my lingie friends didn't understand his answer, but then, they had never spent a Sunday nailing staples in a barbed wire fence. Way back in the States, when we signed up for the army, we had raised our hand and swore we would. Now it was too late to holler, "Kings-X, I didn't really mean it."

Maybe it's difficult for a civilian to understand, but the operative word in 'military intelligence' is often 'military'. Far from the glamorous world of James Bond and George Smiley, electronic operations generally involve long hours of painstaking work to capture a few golden nuggets of covert intelligence. When they are not camped at some dangerous perimeter, soldiers in military intelligence generally work alongside regular infantry units, often enduring the same rough circumstances and dangerous times. Fear of what is to come, relief at overcoming deadly adversity , the joy of living through another day—these are emotions shared by all soldiers.

Coming Ashore

By R. W. "Butch" Williamson

I was with the 330th, and we went across the Pacific to Vietnam by boat. The sea wasn't always calm as plate glass and some of the troopers got sick, but aside from that it was pretty uneventful. When we finally reached Qui Nhon harbor, we were off-loaded into an LST (I guess that stands for Landing Ship Tank…whatever, to an army guy it was just some big ol' navy landing craft, little more than a flat, open boat with big engines to propel us through the surf.) They crammed over 250 GIs from the 330th on that LST, plus a few from some Phy Ops Battalion.

Of course, you never know what to expect when you land like that. They don't tell you anything, and you can't see over the lip of the LST, so you're just sitting inside a big tub waiting for them to crank down the ramp in front so you can run onto the land. We'd been authorized by our company commander to secure a magazine with live ammo in our M-14's, and so that gave us pause for thought. We were ready for action. Still, none of us much liked the M-14, and this was even before they'd proven unreliable in combat. Combat troops always seem to know; the marines were already calling them *Elephant Guns*, probably because they were on their way to extinction...or maybe would help us on our own way.

As we puttered away from the mother ship in our LST, you could feel the tensions mount among the troopers, and nervous butterflies-in-the-stomach feelings continued to rise as we neared the shore.

Our big flatboat finally hit the sand and came to a stop. We were real quiet and thoughtful as the flat ramp in front of the LST cranked down. We peeked out in apprehension. And then we saw him! A naked little Vietnamese kid who couldn't have been more than two, squatting on the beach taking a dump. I thought, What an appropriate introduction—welcome to Vietnam!

GOAT STORIES

By Don Collins

When I arrived at the 409th in February 1967, they had three goats, two male and one female. I'm not sure, but I believe that lamb chops was the driving force behind the goatherd...or whatever they call young goat meat. But it was a disappointment. The males were pretty horny and would screw anything, each other, tent poles, trees...in fact, they would screw anything but the female. Everybody was kind of bummed out about that. The word went around that with millions of goats in the world we had to get the two queer ones.

The goats would butt anyone who wasn't paying attention. One day, one of the guys was bending over and the goat nailed him right in the back of his knee, dislocating it. A few days later, the Nancy Sinatra USO show came to camp. We all got the afternoon off to go and see her. It must have been at least 100 degrees, and we were sitting out in the open in the direct sunlight, sweating like pigs. This guy's knee was still bandaged, and the bandage started irritating him so he pulled up his pants leg to adjust it. Nancy saw this, and, thinking that it was a war wound, sang her way over to him and planted a big old kiss on his face. We were all a bit jealous about it, but we didn't say anything.

Another day, a guy named Madden was coming back from a courier run when he saw the goat we called Homer over by the tents. As a joke, he pointed his M-16 at the goat and pulled the trigger. To everyone's surprise—including Madden's—he fired off a short burst. He was supposed to have cleared his weapon before getting into the helicopter, but he'd forgotten. He missed the goat but took off the earlobe from a sergeant that was in the tent behind the goat. The tent behind the goat was a holding area for new arrivals to the 11th Cavalry. The sergeant had only been there for a couple of hours. Welcome to Vietnam! After that incident, Madden was forever known as Mad Dog Madden.

In general terms, in Vietnam the mission of an electronic spy often involved detecting enemy North Vietnamese troop movements, and good radio intercept operators working at isolated fire bases and even in unsecured secret hide-outs saved thousands of lives. Others were able to locate enemy Viet Cong Provincial and Regional headquarters, which then would be hit with 500 pound iron bombs flown in from Okinawa. Still, the day-to-day life of an electronic spy could seem bloodless and clean, particularly when compared to the constant danger faced by the infantry grunts. Which is why, when the war did rear its ugly head up close and personal, the memories have lasted over the decades and are still fresh and clear as if it all happened yesterday.

THE PAINFUL REALITIES OF WAR

By Dave Parks

It was around May 5, 1968. This was several days into the May Counter-Push that followed the Viet Cong Tet Offensive. I was on a battalion sized Fire Base manned by the 3rd Battalion, 7th Infantry, 199th Light Infantry Brigade. The blond infantryman had been off-loaded from an Armored Personnel Carrier, along with two wounded VC, less than fifteen minutes before. He was lying on a stretcher in front of the Aid Station I was standing in the shade of an OD colored canvas awning that stretched across the front of the Aid Station bunker. I'd been in my PRD-1 site near the Aid Station, and I'd seen the whole thing happen. The APC pulled up, the stretchers were taken out, and then the APC beat a hasty exit. I knew it was going to rejoin a fierce firefight going on about a klick away. I was curious; the trooper might be someone that I knew. I'd lived and worked among these infantry troops, and I'd come to know a few of them. That's why I went over to check things out.

35

Before making my way around to the front of the Aid Station, I passed two wounded VC. They were lying off to the side of the station, exposed to the sun. At first glance, they looked pretty well shot up, and I could see they weren't going anywhere. One was perhaps 35 or 40 years old. The other had to be a teenager. For all I knew, they were father and son. Both wore black pajamas and were covered in mud and blood. Nothing had been done to attend to their wounds.

The younger one was alert, despite having several chest wounds and a left leg that was shot nearly in two below the knee. His glance caught mine as I paused to look them over. I saw the pain in those eyes, and the fear. The older fellow was almost gone. His half-closed eyes were glazed over. Flies worried at both men's exposed wounds, and buzzed over the thick purplish blood that was pooled on their stretchers. Even untrained as I was in medical matters, I could see that, without help, they weren't going to live.

I went on around to the front of the station. I was relieved that the wounded trooper wasn't anyone I knew. Judging by his almost-new boots and fatigue pants, he was new in country. He had blond hair and blue eyes. I was struck by his youth. I was 21, and he looked several years younger than I was.

The medic, who was a staff sergeant, had removed the young trooper's battle dressing, exposing a small, round bluish hole in the middle of his chest. There was no blood. He was just finishing swabbing a dark brownish liquid around the wound. When I stepped up, there was no one else around. The medic glanced up at me and grunted, "Help me roll him on his side so I can check his back."

I did as he asked. There was nothing there. I noticed the kid did not respond to my touch. He was a dead weight.

"Stay WITH me here!" the medic cried. For a split second, I thought he meant me. But he was shouting at the trooper, looking at his face while he rhythmically pushed on his chest. I stepped back. I was at a loss as to what to do. I just watched.

The medic was giving him mouth-to-mouth and pumping his chest in an attempt to move blood around in his system.

"Open your eyes for me! He commanded. "Don't leave me now!" A few seconds went by, and the trooper failed to respond. "You're gonna make it! Just open your eyes for me now!"

The medic grabbed his stethoscope and listened at the silent kid's chest. "Damn it, what's his NAME?" the medic muttered to himself. He looked up at me, "Get over to the TOC and find out where that fucking chopper is!" He pointed toward the Tactical Operations Center. I did, only to be told by a concerned major that one was on the way—but it had to finish dropping off a load of wounded before it could come.

I reported back to the medic. "That don't hardly fucking cut it!" he said. While I was away, two more medics and a captain had joined him. . One of the new medics had taken over on the resuscitation effort, while the staff sergeant applied his stethoscope and felt the trooper's neck for a pulse.

"He's gone, Sarge," the second medic said softly.

The sergeant stopped searching with the stethoscope but did not directly answer. He got up, turned his back and stepped away. He kicked at the dirt at his feet and shouted, "FUUUUCK!"

I didn't know him, but it hit me hard when I realized the trooper wasn't going to make it. There was a lump in my throat and I felt numb. I walked back over to my own site and sat down in the shade of my shelter half, replaying the whole thing in my mind's eye. I found it hard to believe he was dead. It seemed so final and cruel. A while later, when I made myself look back over at the Aid Station, I saw the medics were putting the trooper into a dark green body bag. They lifted his stretcher and placed it crosswise on a jeep, and then drove off toward the chopper pad.

Sometime later, I heard the jeep return. When I glanced back over, I noticed the two VC were still lying beside the station. I got up and went over to them, expecting to find them dead. The older fellow was dead now. His eyes were filmed over, but still open in death. The young one was alive, but not nearly as alert as before. As I approached, his eyes again locked briefly into my gaze. I felt the need to do something for him. I don't know, I guess I thought the medics had forgotten these two.

I went back to my site and got my canteen. I returned, intending to move the VC out of the sun and give him some water. Then I thought maybe I'd better clear this first with the staff sergeant. I wasn't sure if water was the right thing to give him, and I was still wondering why nothing had been done for these two.

I found the medic inside the bunker.

"What are you going to do for those two VC outside?" I asked. "One of them looks like he's already dead..."

"Fuck those gooks!" he swore at me, his voice rising. "Leave them the fuck alone. They can just hurry up and die, 'cause I'm not touching the filthy bastards!"

I was surprised to get this reaction from the same man, who had cried over the death of the young trooper, but he left no room for doubt; that was his final word on the subject of the wounded VC. I was confused, and unsure what I personally should do. I went back around to the side of the bunker. I felt intimidated both by his reaction and my ignorance of medical procedures. Yet I found myself standing there next to the remaining wounded VC with the feeling that I should try something.

As I looked down on the dying man, I realized that the medic knew full well their situation. In fact, he was allowing these two men to die. In some twisted way, it was his payment to the dead American. The young VC's eyes seemed duller now, and his wounds were crawling with flies. I knelt down beside him and tried to brush off some of the flies, but it really didn't do any good.

"Screw the medic," I muttered to myself as I pulled the VC's stretcher into the shade. I ripped a square of cloth from the dead VC's shirt and wet it with water from my canteen. I wiped off the teenager's forehead, upper chest and arms. Again, this didn't seem to do much good. I poured some water on his head. I decided against giving him a drink, thinking it would probably drown him. Nothing I'd done seemed to do any good. I felt frustrated and helpless.

Looking up, I spied the captain who had been around earlier, now smoking a cigarette over near the TOC. I went up to him.

"Sir," I said, "one of the VC who came in with that trooper is still alive. He looks like he's going to die if something isn't done, and the medic says he won't touch him."

The Captain gave me a long, hard look. He glanced over to the aid station, and then back at me.

"If I were you, Specialist, I'd keep my goddamned nose out of it. The sergeant over there is in charge, and you just might need his services some day."

"But, sir—"

"Let him run the aid station any damned way he sees fit."

I could see he was thinking that he himself might some day also need the medic's services. Not really someone you wanted to make your enemy.

With that response, I had to recognize there was nothing more I could do. I gathered up my defeat and returned to my own little corner of the war. And by sundown the young VC was dead.

I've lived with the events of that day for over thirty years now. I'm sure I won't forget any of that until the day I die. For me, each Memorial Day, that young trooper is the image of all the American Dead. Mention someone dying in Vietnam, and his image is the one I see. Beyond that, his face and that of the young VC return to haunt me with some degree of regularity. No one else can see them, of course. Sometimes they put me to sleep. Sometimes they visit me at dawn, before anyone else is awake. Sometimes, I see one or the other of them dining in a restaurant or passing me on the street. The blond trooper represents my *survivor guilt*; he died while I didn't. The teenage VC is my *personal guilt*; I don't know exactly what I could have done, but I should have moved heaven and earth to do more for him. And so to this day I still feel I failed him, as well.

In the early 1960s, the ASA established a major listening post on Tan Son Nhut Airbase, just west of Saigon. This was the 3rd Radio Research Unit (3rd RRU), housed at Davis Station in a rustic enclave built by the French in the days of black overhead fans before brick block barracks and heavy air conditioning. By 1964 there were 17,500 U.S. military advisors in-country, and when off-duty, the enlisted soldiers of the 3rd were encouraged to go downtown wearing civilian clothes and without weapons to show that the Americans were present in force and unafraid. Those above the rank of E-5 (the lowest grade of sergeant) were allowed to live off-base. At that time, Saigon was a boisterous city; some frequented the bars and the nightclubs, others went to the racetrack, visited the gambling pits or chanced the opium dens. Some of those who worked the swing or night shifts found time in the day to get a job, to start a romance or a family, or to try their hand in the thriving black market. The Vietnamese Piaster was trading at an official rate of 79 to the U.S. dollar, but if you had dollars, Johnny, the East Indian who ran Johnny's Bookstore downtown near the Edan Arcade would give you 200 to 250, depending on the daily rate.

GOOD TIMES AT
THE HAPPY JACK PLATTER SHOP

By John Klawitter

Once, in that very long-ago time when I was playing spy in Saigon, I met a Scotsman at the Bristol Bar, which, if my memory serves me correctly, was on the Street-of-Flowers near Le Loi Street. This drunken Scott spoke with such a burr that I could hardly understand him, yet he insisted he was a radio announcer. He was a rrrrrrr-adio jock, mon. What's more, he was leaving in three days for the highlands (Scottish, not Vietnamese), and if I wanted his job, it was mine. Well, Ba Muoi Ba is one of the more powerful beers in the Orient, and as the evening wore itself into a pleasant blur, a career in radio seemed a really nice idea.

The next morning, I staggered out of bed, groped for my shoes and slept in the cab all the way down Pasteur Street to the radio station. Wonder of wonders, the ebullient Scot was there, just like he said he'd be. He walked me around and introduced me as their new radio personality. Then he dragged me into the booth and we were on the air.

This was a couple of years before Adrian Cronauer had his *Good Morning, Saigon* show, and I wasn't on Air force Radio, either. This was the real thing, VTVN–*native radio*. Our signature was a scratchy 78 rpm of the William Tell Overture swiped from the Canadian broadcasting System, and the girls who spun my platters wore slit-skirted ao-gai and ducked under the table whenever they heard the low rumble from the B-52's shellacking the provinces, convinced it was the ghosts of their dead ancestors.

I called my show *The Happy Jack Platter Shop*: I'd do the news, and then records that I'd mostly scammed from GI buddies. The news was a little complicated, though the stories came clacking off the teletypes from AP and Reuters just like they do in newsrooms around the world. But at VTVN we had Vietnamese government interpreters who translated everything to Vietnamese, then scissored out offending passages. The remainders were tossed back to the station interpreter, Mr. Van Nguyen, who translated it back into mind-numbing, chop-socky English. I'd get about 20 desperate minutes to smooth the most obvious craters, and then I was on the air.

Van Nguyen was a little guy with heavy dandruff, sour-whiskey-and-cigarette breath and a small potbelly hanging over the belt-line of his truly cheap suits. I'd known him about a week when he started bugging me for a Pentax. He would be happy even with the smaller Pentax, the less expensive one without the wonderful zoom lens that might make his career.

This one camera, and he would never, ever bother me for anything ever again from the PX, except possibly for some hairspray for his wife and maybe a few chocolate bars for his kids.

I was managing to keep my temper with him, but just barely, when the weak Phan Uy Quat government was overthrown. The cabbies were still running–hell, I heard they ran right through the Tet Offensive–and so I was able to flag a ride over to the station. I passed ARVN tanks in the streets and machine gun nests at corners some military genius had decided were strategic.

The newsroom was deserted, but there was a stack of neatly clipped translations on my desk. If possible, they were even more nonsensical than ever:

[blank space] farm crops [blank space] the cooler weather. [enormous blank space] resulting in lower prices.

[blank space] new American comedians [big blank space]

Nothing at all about the collapse of the government.

Still, Van Nguyen had clearly been and gone. At least I wouldn't have to listen to his miserable whining about the camera he wasn't going to get. I poured a bitter cup of coffee, scooped up the tattered copy and headed for the booth. Before I knew it, William Tell was jangling in my ear, and then I was picking my way through the news. I turned the cut-up farm story into an informative discussion of the pineapple industry, and went on to do a color piece on the Smothers Brothers, those happy, bumbling folk-singer comedians.

Hey, no problem, this show was nearly in the bag. I had my feet up and was into the music side of The Platter Shop–I remember Peter, Paul and Mary were singing "Lemon Tree"–when a squad of ARVNs burst through the door into the room where the turntables and the jittery co-gai were spinning and started waving their machine guns around in the air.

Boy soldiers who should have been in high school. One of them figured out the magic of the soundproof double doors and made his way into the booth where I was. He jabbed his machine gun at the ceiling and said in almost inaccessible English, "You say Ong Quat a filthy pig?"

"Ahhhhhh….nooooo….," I replied.

This didn't seem to make him happy. It probably was the wrong answer.

"You say Ong Quat a filthy pig?," he repeated, turning the machine gun in a somewhat more operational way toward my face.

"Ahhhh, maybe I did say something…" I stammered.

His face darkened and he slammed the safety off. I could see this kid hadn't been to Buddhist Patience School.

And then, by some miracle, the wonderful little Van Nguyen was there, stepping in between us. He went on for a while in his singsong way, and then turned to me.

"A small mistake," he shrugged. "This youngster with gun here, he want you to say Ong Quat is a filthy pig." Van Nguyen gestured encouragingly toward the mike, which was clicked off because Peter, Paul and Mary were still singing. "He not know we on air or not."

"Ohhhh…," I said, clearing my throat as I stumbled over to my chair.

After the show, one of the kids in khaki took a group shot of us with his battered little Kodak, and I even signed an autograph on the back of a crumpled napkin. I waved goodbye and walked swiftly down the big marble staircase. And then I was out the front door and hailing a cab, just happy to still be sucking air.

That afternoon–and I would have done it sooner, but the PX didn't open until noon–I ran over and bought my dear friend Van Nguyen his Pentax. Not the cheap model–the expensive one with the big black zoom hanging on the front that just might make his career.

Vietnam is a moody country, full of mystery and old bones. After centuries of violence and cruelty, some have noted in their culture a tendency to become accepting of atrocity and even accustomed to war. The Viet Cong came and went by night, committing acts of horror to terrorize the population and then vanishing by dawn. To those in the ASA whose day job was about as dangerous as a clerk's or a mechanic's, standing guard by night would bring many of them as close as they might ever come to the elusive enemy.

NIGHT MOVES

By Gary Morin

It was late Spring in 1971 and I was with the 371st ASA Unit, which at that time had personnel numbering about a hundred. We were stationed at Camp Gorvad, which unhappily got its name when Pfc Gorvad became the first casualty suffered by the 1st Cavalry when they moved down from Anh Ke. Gorvad was located on a former Michelin plantation, about an hour and a half's drive north of Saigon. You took Route 13 out of Bien Hoa, and we were about 10 miles from the Cambodian border.

That area had red clay soil, sticky when wet, which it always seemed to be. We were just far enough north to get the northern monsoons and far enough south to get the southern monsoons, so there wasn't much of a dry season. The terrain was flat and the rubber trees in our company area weren't too healthy.

The 1st Cav was assigned to tactical control in that region, and Gorvad was the forward HQ for the Cav. We had a field hospital, airstrip and a battery of artillery, as well as the 1/9th (Buffalo Soldiers) and 2/7th (Custer's old unit). There was a Military Intelligence company next door to ours, as well as the division history group. Some reporters from Stars &

Stripes shared our mess hall, and we had a pretty well stocked PX, considering we were that far out in the boonies.

My usual job was an 05H, a ditty bopper. But you know the army; everyone is issued a weapon and expected to know how to use it, and everyone of lower rank has to stand guard duty. At Gorvad, my turn to stand guard came up every three to four weeks.

One night when I'd pulled guard duty, I was assigned to a bunker on the road to the Mayor of Phuoc Vinh's residence, a French Colonial concrete mansion that was also located on the camp. It was a clear night and we were on green alert, so we weren't really expecting trouble.

The bunker itself was about 50 meters inside the base perimeter, and there was a telephone pole about 25 meters or so outside the perimeter. I recall it was sometime after we got our midnight chow delivery when I looked out and saw somebody climbing that pole. I couldn't be sure, but it looked like somebody in black pajamas. The streetlight was dim, and at that distance it was hard to tell who it was, or even if it was a man or a woman.

It did seem weird, but we didn't know what to think of it. A person climbs a telephone pole in the middle of the night and starts swinging around up there. And then we heard noises, sounding like *ping, ping, ping!*

We jumped down into the bunker to get some solid earth between us, and looked out just in time to see the pole going down. It was hard to get illumination on the subject, as the pop flares refused to go up straight the way they were supposed to. They just shot off in spirals, even falling into other bunkers further along the line. We called Guard Control, but they didn't seem interested in what we saw.

With the gate closed for the night, we couldn't investigate until dawn. As soon as the sun started to give us a little light and the gate was opened, we ran out to the fallen pole. It was one of those concrete jobbies the French had put up before we took over. This looked to be a very old pole, like it had been there a long time. There was no evidence of explosives, nor any evidence that any tools had been used—yet the pole was neatly sheered off at the base.

So you tell me how somebody dressed in black pajamas managed to break off a concrete pole at the bottom while being up at the top at the same time. I think I'm a fairly smart fellow, but to this day, I can't figure it out.

The Viet Cong and their buddies from the North had their own electronic spies, and once they knew of the 3ʳᵈ RRU on the airbase at Tan Son Nhut, it became a prime target for terrorist attack.

It's Not Like You Think

By James G. Scheffler

You can deny it if you want, particularly if you've never been there. It's easier to deny or to put down something you never experienced. But the truth is, there's a certain rush, a high, a feeling of personal elation that you can get by living through a dangerous and life-threatening time. I've felt it, and I'm neither proud nor ashamed of my feelings. It just happened, and I was there to experience it. Of course, I'm glad I made it through, and I feel sorry for those who didn't. I suppose you would, too…if you had been there with me.

The day was 13 April 1966, and I remember it well because it was the day that both the Tan Son Nhut Airbase and myself officially came under fire for the first time. I say officially, because I'd personally been shot at before, and, of course, the VC were always firing at planes from the tree line and trying to send in sappers to blow up things. Tan Son Nhut is just on the edge of Saigon, but we'd been restricted to post for several months because the Buddhists were agitating in the streets on a regular basis. Vietnam! There's a country that just couldn't get it together!

The NCO Club at Davis Station was having severe beer shortages, which meant they were limiting everyone to only two bottles. (Those who know me today will recognize that I always buy two bottles at a time, just in case.) A shortage was one thing, but then the club ran entirely out of beers. I was young and headstrong and saw this as an entirely unacceptable situation. Fortunately, we had a reserve supply. We'd stashed a few left-overs under the sandbags of the bunkers where we would hang out after the club closed. But those didn't last too long, so we were getting pretty antsy.

To make matters worse, our Commanding Officer, Major Beaupre, had heard of some of my earlier antics to get off base, and had a standing order that no one was to get out of the gate without his personal written order. You can imagine our relief when, on the 13th of April, the restrictions were lifted. Everybody who wasn't on shift immediately signed out and went downtown. When I'd held formation at 1530 hours, prior to heading out to White Birch, I did it out of sight of the orderly room, and with good reason. When we finished our trick, most of us went immediately to the club and downed a few. Then we bought a couple cases of Budweiser to take with us to the Davis Station theater. This was an open-air building with a roof, big enough so they could project old movies. They also held Sunday chapel there, for those who wanted to attend.

We were heading over that way with our beers when I felt a sudden call of nature. There's nothing more insistent or forceful than the Oriental trots, and I headed immediately for the latrine while the other guys, including Sp 5 Don Bray, went on to the theater. Not only was I racked with dysentery, I had to put up with the fact that the fellows were going to have a big head start on me with the Budweiser.

I was sitting on the porcelain throne in absolute misery when I heard THAT sound—the distinctive thunk of mortars firing. I'd heard them before, but the outgoing sound had always been louder than the impact. Not this time!

I didn't know what to do. I shouldn't stay, but I couldn't go. I sat there, trying to hurry through my bout with the trots, while five or six tubes cranked out about twenty rounds each per minute. Fortunately most of them were landing out on the runway, just beyond our fence, while some seemed to be landing on Camp Alpha, the replacement and transient center, which was even further away.

I heard one really loud one and realized it had hit about twenty feet away! I could hear the fragments hitting the wooden boards on the outside of the building. I found out later that the round had hit the edge of a concrete sidewalk, spattering sharp concrete chunks and shrapnel everywhere. If I was unwilling to admit it before, I recognized that it was time to get up!

I've heard that a near-death experience will sober you up, but that wasn't the case with me. Maybe I'd had more than a few at the club. I moved out of the latrine and crouched behind one of the large metal storage Conex boxes that were scattered around the area. Drunk as I was, I thought it might be cool to pick up a cheap Purple Heart, so I deliberately stuck my arm out beyond the edge of the Conex. But then it occurred to me that there was nothing in particular preventing a round from landing BEHIND me. It was one of those things that kinda makes you go "hmmmm"…you know? With that thought, I figured I'd do well to find a better cover, and took off like a big-assed bird up the company street.

By now I had become somewhat of an instant mortar expert. I realized that you could tell if the round was coming in your direction if you could hear that little "sh-sh-sh" at the top of its trajectory. And in that moment, I heard the distinctive little "sh-sh-sh"!

I jumped into the only ditch I could find. Unfortunately, it proved to be the benjo ditch, the little canal that carried half-processed human waste away from the latrine. While I huddled in the awful smelling liquid, a half dozen more rounds came in, wounding six or seven more people from our unit. As soon as this latest barrage stopped, I ran to the nearest bunker and jumped in feet-first. The guys in the bunker did not welcome me, but there wasn't anything they could do about it.

After a while there were no more mortars. I could hear the sound of small arms fire going off around the perimeter, so I started back to the barracks to get my M-16. It was at about this time that I remembered that Don Bray had headed for the theater with all our beers. I figured to let the rest of the army fight the war, and headed for the beers.

Don was sitting there with a beer in hand and a smile on his face. "What took you so long?" he grinned. He pointed out that there was a new guy in the theater, some guy who had only gotten to the unit earlier that day. The poor fellow was trying to hide on the floor. I dragged him out from behind some cardboard boxes by one foot and asked him if he wanted a beer.

"N-n-no," he stuttered. "D-d-does this happen all the time?"

"Not really," I replied. "This is the first time ever."

"I-I-I can't believe that!" He boogied out of the theater, heading for the nearest bunker.

Don and I sat there drinking beers and watching the chaos develop after the danger was all over. You know the army, "Turn those lights out!" followed by "Get those God dam lights on!" Don had already been to the arms room, where our army issue weapons were locked up. No one could find the armorer, and no one else had keys to the arms room. (Can anyone spell "Pearl Harbor"?)

"Not to worry," Don said. "There aren't any VC units nearby with enough strength to hit us on the ground."

"What about the gunfire?"

"It's all from U.S. issued weapons. I can tell from the sound. It's ARVN's, shooting ghosts in the dark."

We sat in the theater and drank our beers, while all around us people were running this way and that like chickens with their heads cut off. Finally, a young lieutenant showed up and glared at us, "What the hell are you two doing?"

"We were told to guard the theater, Sir!" Don barked back at him.

He looked suspicious, but he wandered off, looking for other fires to put out. Talk about fires, there suddenly was a huge explosion in the near distance, and for a while the night sky flared like glaring red day. It turned out to be about a half million gallons of fuel, and it burned for a week. The VC also blew up one of AFN's television-transmitting Constellations, the old prop-jobs with three vertical stabilizers.

After everything quieted down, we grabbed the remaining case of beer and headed back to our barracks. It was there that we found out that one of the guys from our barracks had been hit pretty badly. He was pumping blood all over the place from his femoral artery, and from his mouth due to a puncture in his lungs. He'd already been evac'd, and everyone thought for sure he was a dead man, but it turned out he survived. One of the half dozen others who were wounded was a Jewish Navajo Indian named Lieb. He'd gone to Saigon that night, and was virtually passed out in his sack when we got hit. His legs were sprayed with shrapnel, and he didn't even wake up. It wasn't until around dawn that someone woke him up, thinking he was dead because of all the blood—and he STILL didn't know he had been wounded until he got out of the sack. He was so embarrassed by this that he had to be given a direct order from Major Beaupre to show up for the awards ceremony to get his Purple Heart.

And, most important of all, one of our guys, Sergeant Donald Daugherty, lost his life in the engagement. The round that landed twenty feet away while I was in the latrine, the same round that sprayed Lieb's legs with shrapnel, killed Sergeant Daugherty. He was coming out of his barracks when the mortar hit just barely on the edge of the concrete. One fragment cut his jugular vein and he bled to death moments later. If the round had hit in the dirt, most of the explosion would have been absorbed, but who knows, you've got to call it just one of God's little jokes.

That's the way war is. It takes one and leaves another and there's no reason. For 05H Sergeant Daugherty, who came from San Diego and was 29 at the time, that sudden mortar attack meant the end of his life. For me, not knowing anyone in our unit had died, it was a break in the monotony of army routine, an emotional rush and an unforgettable life experience. It's complicated, because one of our own died here, and so it's taken me over 30 years to figure this out. The truth is, in those heightened moments when mortars were bursting and explosions were lighting the night sky, I felt more alive than I've felt before or since.

It's a common misconception that the Vietnam Conflict was fought by illiterate black enlisted men and war-loving white officers. The army has a way of bringing together different people from all segments of our society. Some volunteered eagerly for Vietnam, believing it was their patriotic duty. Others reluctantly hitched up their web belts and marched into the fray. Overall, it is safe to say the stereotypes in movies like Full Metal Jacket, Apocalypse Now *and* Platoon *were part of a far more diverse—and intelligent—brew than you may have been led to believe.*

REVEREND LONG'S MISSION

By Carole Scott

War is a tangled bit of business, and not always what you see on the nightly news. During the Vietnam Conflict, young tourists from Europe would occasionally hike the road from Saigon west to Phnom Penh, out for a youthful lark and seemingly oblivious to the dangers. Usually, if they took a bus and traveled by day, they made it through without incident. American civilians—construction contractors, teachers and U.S. government employees were sprinkled around the country, and Christian missionaries were everywhere. These were uncertain times, yet these people felt they could earn a living, or perhaps follow a calling in Vietnam.

In late 1966 or early 1967, when we were stationed in Pleiku with the 330th, Lee Taylor and I met up with a Reverend Long, a missionary with the Christian Alliance Missionary Program. If you were on the main street in Pleiku, heading west, and you made a left and then at the next street made a right, you would be at *Blow Job Alley*. And, ironically situated across the street from this haven of sin was the Reverend Long's missionary compound, including his *Tin Lanh* (Protestant) Church. The compound was very pastoral, with green grass and trees.

Lee and I were invited to Reverend Long's house for dinner. To our surprise, an American family greeted us, including the Reverend's wife and two young daughters. We had a great time, including a good American home-cooked meal and great company.

The Reverend mentioned that someone at the Pleiku Army Airfield had contacted him about a message or document they couldn't decipher. The way he described it, it was in Vietnamese telegraphics. Lee and I looked at each other and said, "Oh really," and left it at that. You never know where allegiances lie, even with Christian missionaries, and our security clearances rested heavily on our shoulders.

The Reverend ministered to several tribes of Montagnards—the Bru, the Jarai and the Branar were among them. He had opened a leprosarium in Cheo Reo, which was to the southwest. He was a pragmatic man; when he needed concrete for construction, he found the only way he could get some was on the black market from the ARVN Catholic Chaplain (who probably got it from the military).

All in all, it was a memorable dinner and Lee and I enjoyed the Reverend Long's company. Years went by, and ten years later, I heard that the North Vietnam army had killed several missionaries during the communist takeover in 1975. I had feelings of fear for the Reverend Long and his family. In May of 1975 I went to Indiantown Gap Refugee Camp as a translator. I was amazed to see a tall Anglo walking into the theater where we started the initial in processing. It was Reverend Long! He and his entire family had managed to get out before everything crashed, and about 50 of the Montagnards that he'd ministered to also got out. He hadn't been worried; he'd put his faith in God, believing He would provide for them all. His major regret was that he'd almost finished translating the New Testament into Branar before the overthrow.

ASA personnel stationed in Saigon were often envied for their easy access to the bars, the girls, the nightlife of the city. But terrorist bombings were commonplace, and there were no safe areas. Bombs that killed and wounded Americans went off at picnic baseball games, in motion picture theaters, in cafes, bars and restaurants. Americans were sniped at from rooftops. Grenades were tossed from passing motorbikes and cars, or from passersby into jeeps and trucks. It did discourage some of the guys from leaving the relative security of Tan Son Nhut (though explosive devices also found their way to the base restaurant, and Davis Station became a target for hit-and-run mortar and rocket attacks.)

The official policy at the 3rd RRU gradually changed to discourage the casual forays into the big city. But there were some irascible spirits that couldn't be put down. One of these was an ex-car thief from New Jersey who had recovered from his wounds in Korea and now was serving as a linguist in Vietnam.

GETTING BLASTED

By Jack Waer

I've forgotten the exact date, but looking back it seems to me it was in the spring of 1965. My trusty Villiers was on the fritz with timing problems. I had been working on it for a few hours when I gave up in frustration. Since the Enlisted Men's Club at Davis was only about 30 or 40 yards away, I yielded to the temptation and sauntered over for a drink or five. Traffic Analyst Ken Gill was in his usual spot already, positioned firmly down at the end of the bar, drinking a rum-and-coke and pursuing his favorite pastime, reading a book. I'll bet he read a thousand paperbacks during his tour...ahh, but I digress. I perched on a stool next to Ken, ordered a bourbon with a beer chaser and tried to engage him in some sort of real-world conversation. Ken grunted at me in his usual gregarious manner and went badck to his book. I sighed and gave up on the effort. I had another bourbon and wandered over to the corn crib and shower for a 5S. For those of you who don't remember (or don't know) a 5S is a shave, shit, shine, shampoo and shower.

I was neatly spruced up but had no personal transportation, so I trudged to the gate in front of Davis where I caught a dong cart to the Tan Son Nhut main gate. There I hailed a cab and departed for the pleasures of the city. I decided to go to the American Bar and hoist a few or ten. It was early evening, as I recall.

The American Bar was a favorite place, and I sat there for a while drinking 33 Beer. In fact, as I remember it, I was well on my way to a fine evening of getting blasted. And then, as usually happens when one drinks beer, I began to feel the urge to pee. In that crazed logic that sometimes accompanies a military drunk, I remember thinking that *I must be drinking Air Farce beer, since I seemed to drink only one and then P38.* Bad pun. You can see I was in the middling stages of getting a good drunk on. And that's when I started to argue with myself.

"I think I'll order another beer and go pee."

"Naww, I'll go pee and then order another beer."

"Naww, I'll go across the street, pee and order another beer."

"Naww, I'll go across the street, order a beer and then pee."

Decisions, decisions, decisions. I couldn't make up my mind…and procrastination nearly killed me.

I finally decided that, when in doubt, order a beer and go pee. So I did that. I ordered another beer, paid for it and went in the back room to take a pee. Those of you who may remember the American Bar know the pisser was a cramped, closet-like affair, little more than chicken wire walls with thin plaster over them, and the ubiquitous footprints on the terra cotta floor outlining where one had to stand to arc the perfect trajectory into the hole in the floor.

I was standing there steadying myself with one hand while I tried to unzip with the other—when there was a terrific explosion! The plaster on the latrine walls let loose and imbedded little bits of itself in my face and arms. There was dust and flying debris everywhere.

"Inconsiderate bastards!" I muttered. There was total silence from the bar; my problem was that my urge to pee had now reached the critical stage. This had to be my first priority. I finally freed myself and was in the first stage of ecstasy when there was a second violent explosion!

With this new explosion the terra cotta floor broke and I free-fell straight down into a 55 gallon drum of waste. *Oh, joy of joys!!* All thoughts of peeing fled and, with my dick still hanging out, I struggled to hoist myself out of the mess. I could hear the sound of sirens approaching in the distance, and finally there were some voices from the bar.

"Holy shit, what a mess!" One voice said.

"Looks like satchel charges," another offered uncertainly.

"Anybody alive?" a third voice asked.

That seemed to me like a particularly unnecessary question.

"Get me the fuck out of here!" I screamed.

A couple of MPs appeared in the doorway. One look at me and they started laughing. Just what I needed, MPs with a sense of humor. After seeing that my shirt was relatively unsoiled, they took me by the arms and hauled me out. Too bad for them, but my dick was still armed and ready and I still had to pee. This I did, spraying the area like the fountain of youth. They were not impressed, but by now ambulances had arrived and they moved off to help carry out the dead from the bar proper.

Because of my extremely soiled condition and ungodly smell, I was relegated to the back floor of a deuce-and-a-half truck and driven to the Saigon Navy Hospital. When we arrived at the hospital, the medics took one look at me and got out the hose. They hosed me down in the back of the truck and then hauled me out by my feet and hosed me down again on the cobblestones. After that I was stripped naked and sprayed a third time before I was finally brought into the emergency room. There it was concluded that I had a concussion and many little pieces of plaster in me. It must have been somewhat worse than I remembered, because I spent ten days in there before I was healed up enough to be sent back to Davis Station.

Yes, some people died but I didn't. You have to keep your perspective about these things, try to find the amusing moment in all the loss and pain and sadness or I suppose it could drive you crazy. I like to remember it this way: the most horrible part of the whole adventure was that my room was on the third floor of the hospital. By chance it happened to be across the alley from a bar, and on the third floor of that building was a very loud and busy whorehouse…so I was very horny by the time they let me out.

While Vietnam could be a very scary and uncertain place, only a fraction of the soldiers stationed there were assigned to combat duty, to search and destroy patrols, to prowl the bush where every step might be on a poisoned punji stake or a deadly bouncing betty. Even the intelligence personnel stationed in remote listening posts like Phu Bai (in Central Vietnam, a few miles from the border with North Vietnam) were thankful for the relative security of their assignments . Vietnam was a half-world away from being Stateside, and light years separated from the sense of peace and calm they all had taken for granted back home.

THE MESS HALL AT PHU BAI

By Danny Owen

During the Tet Offensive of 1968, Steve Clayberg, Bill Rucker, a few other guys and myself were sitting around the mess hall. We were bullshitting, trying to relax and avoiding returning to work. Aside from us, the mess hall was empty. Chow time was over and the cooks were in the back, cleaning up and doing whatever cooks do in the kitchen. They would be getting around to it, but they hadn't yet completely cleaned up the chow line.

We were complaining, as soldiers do, about the food, which had been worse since the Offensive had made ammunition a more important commodity than our normal food supplies. In truth, the mess sergeant, who was a big white-haired E-7, did extraordinary things with what little he had to work. He even baked fresh bread; if you held it up to the light and picked the flour beetles out of it, it wasn't bad. Anyway, we were sitting there, full of the fresh and warm food we'd just eaten. We'd even had our choice of tea, coffee or milk.

As I said, Tet was in full swing, but by now we knew the drill. If we heard rockets whistling, we knew they were passing overhead, probably headed for the airport. If they impacted, it was time to head for the trench line. But this was the supper hour (that's dinner for non-Southerners, dinner being the noon-time meal down South) and we weren't too concerned about being hit at that time of day. I will agree with anyone, though, Charley didn't seem to mind what time it was when he hit, just that he seemed to prefer the night.

As we sat there passing the time, a Marine sergeant stepped in through the door. From the look of him, and judging by his rank, I thought he was a career soldier. He surveyed the room, not making eye contact until he looked at me...and that was just a fleeting glance. Perhaps he sensed that I was watching him. I remember I felt a little awed.

He walked past us without another glance. We were in the enlisted side of the mess hall rather than the NCO side, but that didn't seem to matter to him. He wore the regulation Marine cover and green fatigues...no tiger stripes or jungle cammo, just green fatigues. His boots were covered with dried mud that cracked off and dropped onto the floor as he walked toward the chow line. His eyes were light blue. He was a tall man, maybe 6'2", and very lean. I could tell that he was tired, just very, very tired, and yet he carried himself with dignity. Looking at him, it seemed to me that he had seen a lot more than I could at that time conceive of.

There wasn't much left in the chow line, and what was still available was cold by this time. The Mess Sarge would have fixed him something, but he didn't ask. Instead, he ladled different items into the compartments on his tray and poured himself a glass of tea.

After setting his supper down on a table across from where we sat, he sat down and sighed. He just looked at his tray of food for several seconds. We were still laughing and cutting up, seated at our own table across from him, but he didn't pay any attention. I couldn't help but watch him. Up until that time, I hadn't had much contact with combat types. I saw him fold his hands together and bow his head. Although I couldn't hear the silent prayer he was saying, I knew that he was praying. Being raised in the South and in the Church of Christ, I easily could lip-read the word "Amen" at the end of his prayer. After finishing, he began to eat the cold food with slow, deliberate bites. To someone like him, used to nothing more than C rations or LRRP rations, the food we bitched about and took for granted was a feast. He certainly was enjoying it.

Over the years since, I've remembered this simple chance meeting. I've thought about it a lot and often. It has had a definite influence on my life; there he was, a man who had faced death in a lot of different ways, sitting down and blessing the food that I had so often complained about and even scorned. And I've often wondered if he made it back. I pray he did.

Over three decades after the fact, the memories of a tour in Vietnam still are fresh and clear as if it were only yesterday—and in remembering, it's often not the unusual or the unexpected but rather the absolutely commonplace event that comes to mind and sticks and won't go away.

THE BEST CAN OF BEER I EVER HAD

By Dennis St. Germaine

It's funny, the things you remember. We'd just gotten to Vietnam. We processed in-country at Davis Station, and in our off-hours, we drank up the entire supply of San Miguel, which back then was a largely unknown but excellent beer out of the Philippines. I did my share of the imbibing, and so I fully deserved the massive hangover I was carrying around the next day. I remember I almost lost it at breakfast when, expecting a delicious meal of eggs and bacon, I took a big swallow of duck eggs. I gagged, I whimpered, my eyes watered, my hands and feet tingled, the world grew dark. Those delicious-looking eggs sucked!

Soon after, we left Davis Station and found ourselves in an overgrown area north of Saigon. We were part of the 2nd Brigade, First Infantry, and we were stationed in a small village known as *The Widow's Village*, armed with machetes and M14s. The machetes were for cutting down jungle, and the M14s were for—well, you know all about that part.

There we were, chopping down carnivorous shrubbery and slapping ants, filling sandbags and digging deep foxholes with entrenching tools. I have vivid impressions from that time. Sand, dirt, insects, snakes, heat and VC smart enough only to come out at night when it was cool and they could move about without being spotted.

By the end of the second week, after we cleared enough ground, we set up three GP mediums where the enlisted men could bunk. We also set up two HQ tents, one for the two officers and another for the two ranking NCO's.

It wasn't much fun surviving in an unsecured area. We guarded our own perimeter for the first month. We set up two-hour shifts and everyone took a turn on guard duty almost every night. One night, after we'd been there about a week and just before we set up the tents, we were hit by a sapper platoon. We figured they were probably from the 9th VC regiment. It was a memorable moment. There was lots of shooting, and grenades were flung from both sides. I fired a few clips. I just scoped out where I could see the tracers coming from, swung a few degrees to the right, and pumped out rounds.

One of our guys, Roland Scherer, got hit in the forehead with grenade shrapnel. A close call, but it sounds worse than it actually was. When things quieted down, Steve Fox and I took him to the medic tent. They removed the shrapnel and put a small band aid over the wound. We went back to our foxhole and stayed awake until dawn, and three weeks later Roland got his Purple Heart.

We gradually got our camp together. Funny, how the little things stick in your memory. One day about three weeks after we'd been at Davis Station, a Spec 4 came by our area driving a jeep that had a small trailer attached…an honest-to-God beer trailer. He must have been from the newly-arrived field PX, and he had a beer for every man in the det. No ice, and no church keys, but that lone warm Schlitz was as treasured as all those San Miguel's I'd downed at Davis. The only problem was, this was the age before pop-tops, and I had no can opener. Not to worry! Finding this hot Schlitz in my hands, and being the resourceful G.I. that I was, I reached for my dog tags. That's where I kept my P38, universal tool of the infantryman, hanging and clanging from the same chain. Using that small engineering marvel, I made two holes in the top of the hot can and sucked it down. Now I never liked Schlitz, and that brand of beer has long gone to that great beer garden in the sky…but that was one of the best beers I ever drank!

For various reasons, intelligence operatives would extend their tours in Vietnam. And dangerous and difficult as it could be in the bush, some preferred the more relaxed regulations at a remote LZ (landing zone) to life in a secure but up-tight post where a scuffed shoe or badly pressed shirt could mean guard duty or KP (kitchen patrol, mostly peeling potatoes and washing dishes).

A Nug in Di An

By Bruce I. Schindler

It was early afternoon. I was in the club, nursing a beer. I was low on cash, so it looked like a bit of a dry spell until payday. I was the only one in the club other than the guy tending bar, and he'd long since taken to ignoring me. It was the slow time; the guys working nights were still asleep, and those working evenings didn't want to show up to work with too much beer on their breath, and those working days wouldn't be off for a couple of hours yet.

Now there are corner saloons and all sorts of taverns and nightclubs, but, in some respects, the *club* is a military variation on the theme, and most installations and larger units had them. There was, of course, the bar for beer and hard liquor, generally some tables for gatherings, poker games and pinochle, and maybe a small kitchenette serving cold sandwiches. Where possible, the club system was organized along the lines of the military caste system, that is, Officers, Non-Commissioned Officers (NCOs, generally sergeants or higher ranking specialists), and Enlisted all had their own clubs. But with the ASA, which went by the alias *Radio Research* in Vietnam, the main qualification to get in their clubs was a high security clearance, and you might see officers and enlisted men in the same room, though probably at different tables. This was one of those *mixed* clubs, but like I said, there was nobody else but the bartender, so it didn't really matter.

I heard the door open. Turning my head, I saw this guy scoping out the bar. Mostly, he was looking at me. He studied my brand new boots, and then my new uniform, still innocent of patches or rank. He smiled. It was a kind-of predatory, used-car salesman smile. He came on over.

"When'd you get in?" he asked.

"Today," I said.

A friendly smile lit his face. I guess it was clear to him that I was a *nug*, that's army slang for *a new guy*. There are other words for it. *Newk*, pronounced "Nuke". Or FNG, that is, *fuckin' new guy*. But now, here in Di An, I was a nug.

"What unit are you assigned to?," he asked.

"337th," I replied.

He grabbed the next stool and ordered two beers, pushing one in front of me. His name was Harry. He'd been in-country with the 337th RRU (Radio Research Unit) in Di An for about six months. It looked like he was going to clue me in on how things were.

Sitting there, drinking cold beers ordered up by my new friend, it seemed like it might be some fun. After all, he was buying the beer. Harry ordered another round and started in on his guided tour.

He told me the 337th supported the 1st Infantry Division, and that we wore the Big Red One patch, even though we were ASA. Harry talked fast and ran his sentences together in a fashion I found altogether amazing.

"Di An is mostly a military base," he said, "though there's a shit pot of *Mama-sans* working around here, I'm not sure what they all do exactly, but right here now, you see, we're in III Corps, that's about 20 miles from the Bien Hoa Air Force Base, not too far from Saigon, you see, for a fast run in and a hot night on the town, when you can get away, that is." He took a gulp of air. "See, we're in the 337th, and we support the 1st Infantry Division, we wear the Big Red One patch, even though we're ASA." He winked, we were fellow-conspirators in an intelligence deception. Leave it to me, I'll tell you who to look out for, where to go, what to do, the guys to hang out with. I myself got in-country toward the end of the monsoon, but the really old guys say it can rain buckets. They say it can be hot and dusty all night and all day, and then the clouds come in about three in the afternoon and dump two to four inches of rain. Then the sun comes back and turns the place into a sauna. Course, now it's just hot and dusty the whole day."

One of the rules is, when the other guy's buying, you try to do nothing to interrupt the flow. I must have been doing pretty good, because the beers kept coming, and Harry kept right on clueing me in.

"Right here in Di An is the place to stay," Harry said.

"Oh, why's that?" I asked. "Where else could I go?"

"Well," he frowned at the unhappy possibility, "there's another place, Lai Khe, and we've got a platoon up there. Lai Khe is about 30 miles up Thunder Road, that's Viet Highway QL-13, you know, going toward the Iron Triangle, the Fish Hook and the Parrot's Beak...on the Cambodian border. You don't want to go there."

"Why not?"

"Nobody but losers and malcontents go there. Being sent there is a fate you want to avoid at all costs. But don't worry. I'll help you stay clear. Count on me."

"This doesn't seem to be too pleasant, down here in Di An, all flat with no trees and just a bunch of drainage ditches..."

"Don't kid yourself, brother; they don't even have real buildings up there in Lai Khe; the guys just live in tents."

That was true enough. Di An had wooden buildings with metal roofing, and the Operations Building was in a Quonset. But Lai Khe was built on a rubber plantation owned by Michelin. They had lots of shade trees. I knew first hand that platoon in Lai Khe had staked a claim to an area of really large shade trees, and at that time it was like living in a park. What's more, we had nearly all the mission—we functioned with very little organizational aggravation.

Maybe it was the beers, but after a while, it seemed to me that old Harry was building a verbal tower out of matchsticks and hot air. To listen to him, he certainly had been around. It didn't matter what the subject was, Harry was the hero. And gradually he started to get around to it—if I played my cards right, I was going to be his number one right-hand man. I nodded quietly at this, pondering my exceeding good fortune, and Harry ordered another round of beers.

As the afternoon wore on, other unit members started coming in. They glanced at Harry and me, and I could see they took me for his *nug de jour.* Finally, one of the old hands came in, a guy named Pat that I'd known up at Lai Khe early in his tour. Pat had gone back to 337th main in Di An, while I did my best to stay away from the flagpole, you know, preferring the informality of Lai Khe.

"That guy," Harry said confidentially, nudging me and pointing in Pat's direction. "You wouldn't believe it. He's just extended his tour here in the hell-hole another six months!"

Pat got a beer and nodded over to me. "Hey, Bruce, It's been a while."

It had, actually. Pat had left Lai Khe about the time I'd gotten orders for Berlin. To my way of thinking (without having been there), Berlin sounded like another base camp, only without the combat pay. I did my math, and decided the easiest way to get through four years of the Army was to have a month of paid vacation every time I extended six months. Not to mention that the pay was tax-free, and maybe, maybe I might be able to save a life or help shorten the war.

"Hi, Pat," I replied. "I heard you extended. How come?"

Harry acted like he'd just peed on a 220 power line. "Wait a minute," he said, "You know each other?!"

Pat and I looked at each other and shrugged. "Right," Pat said in poor Harry's direction. Then he looked back at me, "Wife send divorce papers…going off to find herself…or something…or someone."

"Bummer," I replied, Harry suddenly becoming irrelevant. But my new-found friend wasn't going to be put off so easily. He stepped between

Pat and myself and gave me an accusing look. "When did you get in-country?" he demanded.

"Today," I said with a deadpan look. "I told you that."

"No! I mean, when did you first get in-country?"

"Well, gee, that's different. I guess about 18 months ago."

"Ohhh…Well, where have you been?" Harry demanded, trying to salvage something.

I gave him my frosty smile. "With the 337th, in Lai Khe."

That seemed to deflate Harry for good, and he slunk away, probably with an eye out for a new crop of nugs. He'd taken good care of my thirst, not to mention my boredom. To this day, I do feel some sense of gratitude for that. I've got to say, Harry, if you're out there somewhere and want to buy some more beers, I can probably find the time to listen to your stories.

Editor's note: The 337th RRU was an ASA Company, Company B of the 313th USASA Battalion, which in turn was part of the 509th USASA Operations Group responsible for covert intelligence operations in Vietnam. The 337th was assigned to support the 1st Infantry Division.

Being a linguist in Vietnam and in military intelligence could be heaven and hell at the same time. Early in the war, before the U.S. military took over and made it 'our war', linguists were relied on in a way that dissolved after the escalation of 1965 increased the U.S. presence from roughly 17,000 troops to a half-million. After the mid-1960s, the emphasis was more on smashing the enemy and less on understanding our allies. Critics of the war will point out that this was always the case, that we never really understood the Vietnamese, friend or foe. Many of those who were actually there in those early years would submit that this wasn't true. The ASA's own army-trained linguists, many of whom had steeped themselves in the culture, religion and history of Southeast Asia, disagreed with the strategic shift and saw in that early move the first unraveling of our possibilities for success.

UP IN THE AIR

By Roger Thurman

Somewhere along the line, linguists came to be known as "Monterey Marys." There are reasons for this. For one thing, it takes up to a year to learn the basics of a language, and many linguists spent 47 weeks at the Defense Language Institute, which is located on the Monterey Peninsula, a supposedly cushy assignment in a pleasant resort by the sea. Also, officers tend to be suspicious of people who know more than they do about anything, and most officers knew little or nothing about the Vietnamese language or people. Then too, the way the war was going, there was less and less love lost between the Americans and their allies, and speaking Vietnamese could be confused with consorting with the enemy. Still, the busy Americans occasionally needed an important document translated or an idea expressed, and in those brief moments full attention was paid as the linguist opened the magic cross-cultural door. Not surprisingly, linguists tended to take a cultural and historical view of the war; they were filled with facts about the unhappy French and Chinese experiences in that sad land, glum histories that made people of rank uncomfortable. Perhaps for this reason, if no other, the linguists had somewhat of a "geek" status and were somewhat unaffectionately called *lingies*.

In the GI parlance of the day, lingies liked to "skate" away from sandbag filling and bunker construction. We were sheltered by the super-secret Army Security Agency, whose hallowed mission and tactical placements could not be transgressed by anyone, including the highest-ranking officers and civilians lacking the proper security clearance and indoctrination. And the ASA regularly scooped normal military intelligence gathering. You can see there were those in the army who did not particularly like the ASA in general or lingies in particular.

Be that as it may, this story concerns one Monterey Mary who had no apparent mission and who avoided having rank and nametags applied to his uniform. The place was Chu Lai, about 80 kilometers south of Danang. It was an airbase and headquarters for the newly reborn Americal Division, whose headquarters perched on a huge bluff overlooking the South China Sea. The place was relatively easy to secure because the sandy, scrubby terrain was protected by a chain of low mountains that gave way to rice paddie3s, sparse villages and Highway 1, which ran north south. The 196th Light Infantry Brigade base camp stood guard to the south and patrolled inland west of the mountains, while the ARVN 2nd Division took care of the northern approach.

The captain faced with the problem of the Monterey Mary with no mission was Captain Mark Galeton. I, of course, was the problem.

Captain Mark had an aquiline brow and West Point training. I always felt he created his own problem when he told me the 408th Radio Research Dot., which was supporting the 196 LIB of American, didn't really know how to utilize my skills.

I thought fast and creatively. "Well," I replied, hardly missing a beat, "why not let me go to the *vile* and polish my language skills...?"

I let the idea dangle out there like a carrot. He seemed to be taking me seriously, so I plunged ahead. "I can keep my ear to the rail. Maybe I can gather intelligence about local VC activities."

"What else?" he queried.

I was on a roll. "I can also serve as an interpreter on medical missions to the surrounding villages." And then I thought of a topper, "And I'll also put in some time at the Chu Lai POW cage, to observe interrogation language and technique!"

That last one struck a chord somewhere in the man. "Okay," he agreed cheerfully. "You work on that!" He waved goodbye as I stepped out of the door of his hooch and into lingy heaven. Here I was, given free rein to mingle with the natives, and I had the captain's blessing! I immediately decamped for the ville, which was a mile or so down the road, making sure not to tell anyone of the terms of my new job description.

The ville was An Tan, a little market town and bus stop located along Highway 1. It wasn't far from the airbase gates. The grid layout of concrete block buildings was not traditional, because many of the residents were refugees or people displaced when they built the airbase. The laundries, restaurants, jewelry shops, dry goods stores and whorehouses seemed to have been constructed in haste, and were largely put together with mortised wood poles, stucco brick and tin-roofs. If there was an anchor to An Tan, it was the imposing whitewashed Catholic church, complete with an orphanage and a school, all housed in a compound set back from the road in the middle of the town. Broad paddies stretched some distance from behind the church to the foot of the mountains. The compound's entrance was next to a dirt town square where taxis and busses exchanged passengers, and busy vendors sold food and goods from carts. There was also a seldom-used outdoor theater along the highway, and a few small and nondescript district office buildings, including a police station.

I began to make contact with the people of An Tan, and so began one of the most amazing experiences of my life. Any casual conversation I might start by the road would inevitably lead to a gathering. I would be asked to sit down. They would bring me some tea, and people would gather to hear me speak. They would murmur, titter and giggle as I struggled with the Central Vietnamese dialect. The Hanoi dialect I had learned was crisp and precise; but at first I could barely comprehend their pronunciations, and their use of terms and phrases I found unfamiliar.

People would ask me for favors, for help in locating a lost relative, or for a job on the base. With no dental care, many traditional peasant Vietnamese chew the betel nut to numb the pain of aging gums and teeth. As these sessions progressed, the betel-nut crowd drew closer. Some looked through the lens of my glasses and then peered around them at my eyes.

"His eyes are really deep-set," someone would crow, to the marvel of the throng. Others would stroke the blond hair on my arms, which must have seemed like fur to the Vietnamese, who mostly only have hair on their heads. The would actually hug me and caress my shoulders, back, chest, stomach and legs, trying to learn more about me in some primitive way by exploring how my body was put together. I was asked many things. What was my family like? What of my home? Was I rich? They seemed to approve when I said I was middle class. No matter what I said, the utterances of "ohhh" and "ahhh" would go through the assembled crowd. They were fascinated when I told them my mother had been married before, and therefore, my older sister was my half-sister. Such an insight into my personal family made me more human, I guess.

Sometimes an older gap-toothed woman with heavy betel breath would smile and ask the most innocent question, which I could not comprehend because of the dialect and her peasant-style slurring. As I apologized for my failure, someone from the back of the crowd would shout, "He speaks grammatically correct, lady, so you have to speak clearly!" Then others would try to rephrase her question more clearly, or make light of her if I had been asked a question they considered dumb, or one I had already answered.

Eventually the sessions would get closer and closer, with too many people clinging to me. Then I'd make my excuses and head for shelter. As often as not, that proved to be the nearest laundry, which generally was a front for a whorehouse. The whorehouses had their own structure; each had a mamma-san who ruled. It seemed that, the stronger the mamma-san, the better it was for business. Many of the girls were young and lovely, but had been sold into the trade to help support their families. At first, I was moved to tears by the inequities, and the many plights which I saw on every side. But I learned to distance myself; nearly everyone, it seemed, was desperate for help, and yet it was impossible to help more than one or two.

I'd never been to a place like Vietnam before, and it affected me deeply. Almost anyone could do anything to anybody and get away with it. In Vietnam the norm was "open season" on the human condition. And it didn't pay to be soft. Woe to anyone who allowed their awareness of the general misery around them to deter their impulse for self-preservation.

My experience in town was wonderful, but after a couple of weeks, my routine began to wear thin with the ditty boys back at the unit, the hard-working Morse code intercept operators who were the soul of our mission. The started to notice the attention that was being paid me by the girls who kept bar at the F Troop Armored Cav's club across the dirt road from the 408th. Jealousy began to rear its ugly head.

I'd just returned from the Chu Lai pole barn PX, having fed my camera fetish with two neat scores—a Nikkormat with no meter and a Nikonos underwater thingy—when my bunkmate, Dave Christmas, said they wanted me in OPs for something. I headed for the corral of vans covered by canvas that made do for our OPs center.

In the OPs hut a skinny lieutenant who gave me a smirk that indicated he had my number confronted me. I knew he didn't like me. I'd gotten on his bad side during a compensatory mission to a Cao Dai village that had suffered a tragic loss. The incident was foolish enough; A drunken G.I. who himself was under indictment for murdering a sergeant was allowed to drive a jeep that was pulling some of the day workers in a trailer attached behind. The G.I. had gone too fast and several of the day workers were thrown from the trailer. The brigade doctor, a wiry major who seemed to care about the native people, called me in to talk to one of the injured, an old man who had been paralyzed with a broken neck. The old man kept repeating something in a dialect I couldn't understand. I later found out that he was asking that no one cut off his ponytail. He was a follower of the Cao Dai religion, and believed that this shock of his hair is the root of the soul, and must never be cut.

Admittedly, our cultures were enormously different, but the Army had not thought out these differences. In typical , go-ahead American fashion, they had built a new school in the village…not realizing that the villagers, who were more interested in food than education, believed the school building was haunted with bad spirits and so permanently tainted that no one was allowed to enter it.

Be that as it may, the old village elder was dying, and I was assigned to go along with the skinny lieutenant to the man's village to pay reparations and to apologize. The lieutenant told me what to say, but as he couldn't really understand what I was saying, I added some embellishments of my own. I remember telling the assembled villagers that it was stupid of the U.S. Army to allow an accused criminal to get drunk and drive innocent civilians. I guess I did get a little carried away, and I went on a bit about my own problems with army life, my distaste for the war, and my hope that their lives could soon be returned to normal.

Somewhere in there, I believe the skinny lieutenant started to get the drift of what I was saying. He shifted uneasily and finally stopped me,

"Come on, Thurman," he said, "let's get out of here. You're sounding like Everett Dirksen, or somebody…"

When I met him in the CO's hut, I knew he was remembering the village incident. There was no love lost between us, that much is sure. He smirked as he explained a special mission that had been devised on my behalf. We were to try airborne voice intercept, he said. I was to accompany an observer pilot on his routine mission. The equipment we were to use was a portable field tape recorder and a small radio. The job seemed ridiculously ill thought out and the equipment outlandishly primitive to be tackling the assignment he outlined, but he was, after all, a lieutenant, and so I didn't say anything. He ordered me to report to a hanger at the airfield, and I gave him the old salute, which meant I would.

The observer pilot proved to be a wiry veteran, a brush-cut blond fellow with a southern drawl and a pair of pearl handled six-guns. We would be flying in an OV-1 Cessna Skymaster, a push-pull prop job of an airplane. I piled my radio gear into the plane and set up as much as I could while he kicked the tires. In a short time we were climbing over the misty mountain range that separated the baked sand of the coastal territory from the badlands. I took a moment to admire the profound beauty of that sparsely settled wilderness. Below I could see the hilly terrain, webbed with a few roads and sprinkled with small villages surrounded by paddies. It felt like I was floating in a moist emerald green expanse. This, I thought, must be something like rural Ireland might appear from the air.

We skimmed the mountaintops for a while. The pilot thought he saw something, and so he gained a little altitude. I got busy, scanning some freqs for a VC voice talk show. This, of course, was totally crazy. Covert messages are sent in code, not jabbered open air over a mike. My job became more and more difficult because we were no longer in level flight. I was apparently only a small part of the pilot's job; he felt he had to check out anything that looked like enemy bunkering or trail activity; he would point a wing at an area of interest and make a very tight circle while marking positions on his maps and entering notes in a log book.

I had to admit he was a consummate professional, the way he managed his little penthouse office in the sky. Even so, I suspected he was having just a hint of pleasure at my inept fumbling with the lap-borne equipment. Each time he'd switch wings to point the other one at the ground, I'd have to start over. We were constantly banking in 45-degree circles while experiencing a steady couple of g's from the tight circling.

Things started to deteriorate for me. The fireball sun seemed to be rotating crazily about the aircraft like an electron from hell. The misty little clouds were now something to duck, and the vibrant green of the terrain was becoming unpleasant. I was finding it impossible to look at the radio dials; the job had reduced itself to becoming one of maintaining my composure. It seemed to me that my pilot was now my jailer and tormenter. He'd occasionally look at me and hand me an airsick bag, shouting with a big smile, "How ya doing?"

It took willpower to keep down the PX dry roasted almonds and the can of tuna I'd gobbled down before the mission. I tried to divert my attention by taking a picture. I reached for my camera. It was the Nikonos, which I'd grabbed instead of the Nikkormat. As I peered queasily through the viewfinder, I was overcome by the absurdity of using an underwater camera to take an airsick tourist shot from a manic airplane that was little more than a target floating above a war zone.

Time passed and I felt worse. As I approached passing out in a faint, the pilot nudged me to put on the cabin headset. It seemed his body language was more alert and serious. He said he'd gotten word we were to break off our current mission and do something else. I was starting to drift into fantasy. *To make your flight more pleasant, ladies and gentlemen, for your listening pleasure, take note of the FM muzak from one side of your headphones. If you need to talk to your pilot, just press the button and he'll hear you. Meanwhile, sit back and enjoy the view while we handle a FAC mission in support of an infantry unit making contact with hostile forces.*

We entered a sweeping dark green valley that had a thin river snaking past little clearings along its banks. There were small huts in the clearings. The muzak (I hadn't been imagining it) was turned off, replaced by a constant chatter from the pilot to the ground forces and to the U.S. Air Force jets that were waiting his word to dispense their fury. We entered a stomach-lobbing dive as the pilot feathered his engines slightly and extended his flaps. It was October, 1967, and we were now listening on one side of our headphones to a broadcast of the Baseball World Series. Our dive steadied and the drone of businesslike war chatter continued in my other ear. The pilot flipped a switch and fired a marker rocket. The recoil from the rocket caused our plane to lose speed. We pulled off-target to circle back…and do it again.

The pilot told the jets to hit his smoke, which they apparently did. Meanwhile, I was using every ounce of concentration to maintain my stomach. I had the feeling that, if I'd spewed gastric juices laced with almond tuna all over his office at this time in his business day he might be tempted to reach for one of his pearl handled pistols and, after dispatching me, blame it on small arms fire from the ground. My head was spinning from the sensory overload. I hunched over and hugged my primitive receiving equipment.

Our mission accomplished, we headed back to Chu Lai, where he set the mosquito-like craft down on the huge, jet-streaked runway. By the time we got to the hanger, I had recovered sufficiently enough to remove my gear from the plane and shake the pilot's hand.

"Didn't need that bag after all, eh?" he observed, one hand resting comfortably on one of the pearly handles of his weapons. He seemed a little perplexed, both disappointed and pleased at the same time, and I had the impression that whether I would lose my lunch or not was the biggest crisis of his day.

"No, sir," I replied, trying for matter-of-fact. "Thanks again for the smooth ride."

I hadn't really accomplished anything, but back at our area, my ditty-bopper bunkmate Dave somehow covered for me. The skinny lieutenant enjoyed hearing what happened, particularly the part about the tapes being entirely blank because I was being tossed around in the sky.

I headed for my bunk to settle my aching head and contemplate what foolish things people do to make a living in a war zone. And the next day I went back to the *ville*.

If you've stayed with the program this far, you have a pretty good idea of the various types of electronic spies and what they have to put up with. Here's a look at one ASA member's recollections from his 12 months in Vietnam.

CLOSE CALLS & OTHER THOUGHTS

By Dave Parks

Introduction

My tour in Vietnam was from November of 67 to November of 1968, and that was thirty-two years ago. Still, to this day, the images of that conflict are indelibly etched on my mind's eye. Here are a few of those images and those stories; some are funny and some ugly, all are true.

Very few Americans ever think about the Vietnam war these days; fewer still know its history, and I find that a sad fact. For me there is no forgetting, I won't allow it while I'm still alive.

When I returned Stateside, to the place we called "The World", I was emotionally numbed, even though I didn't know it at the time. It took years for me to know what had happened to me, and even in the knowing I still couldn't allow myself to feel. I don't think I'm unique in that experience—many of us came back with our feelings shut down to one degree or another. I've been told it's a natural coping mechanism stimulated by the violent deaths witnessed and by the need not to "get too close" to those who might die tomorrow. You wouldn't think it would be so with me. After all, no one in my unit, the 856th RRD was killed, or even scratched during my tour. Still, several friends of mine were lost from the units I worked with within the199th Light Infantry.

One unit, "A" company 2/3 Infantry, was virtually wiped out the night of Tet 68, and I had left that unit three days before. I knew those troopers; they had introduced me to war when I'd lived with them on a small compound in the delta.

That "numbness" I felt lasted for almost ten years, and it took the death of my mother for me to finally feel "normal" emotions again. When my feelings broke through, it was with a drama that I am sure startled all present, it did me. After her graveside ceremony at New Liberty church in the mountains of north Georgia, within sight of where she was born and grew up, I remained graveside until the grave diggers began to shovel clay on top of her coffin. When I saw that, I heaved a big sob and snatched a shovel from one of them and hissed at them to "get the fuck away."

I began to bury her myself. Eventually my sister came up and put her arms around me and I collapsed into a crying heap.

"You don't have to do that" she said.

I replied "You don't understand, I want to do this. I can finally feel something!"

Stories

"A" company 2/3 Infantry in the delta, late November or early December, 1967. My jeep, trailer and I had been commandeered to haul back some bodies from an ambush site a mile or so down the road. A grunt Buck Sergeant was driving and he seemed to know where we were going. A butter-bar Lieutenant sat in the back. I was brand spanking new in-country. I'd been in Vietnam less than three weeks and in the field only a few days. I had been sent there to get my OJT (on the job training) with a fellow known as Hoss, called that because of his uncanny resemblance to the TV character in the Bonanza Series, that was popular at that time. Hoss was nearing the end of his tour and I would be his replacement on the PRD-1 team when he went back to "The World" in a few days. I was doing fine with the OJT-ing, but it was the harsh reality of my little corner of the war that was causing a major re-evaluation of my past sins. I'd started wondering how in hell I had ended up here. I could see the game was played for keeps out here at the edge of the playing field; Americans and Vietnamese died or got the hell shot out of them almost every day in this part of the delta.

I had a lot to learn, and I knew it. My Army Security Agency training didn't cover any of this-death from bullets or shrapnel was only one part of it; there were snakes and other critters roaming the landscape, creatures that would make you just as dead as an enemy sniper.

We drove for a short while as the Sergeant rattled on about his part in the ambush that had taken place earlier that morning. To me, his speech seemed disconnected and jerky, and I couldn't make heads or tails out of most of what he was saying. Maybe it was the way he talked around the big plug of tobacco in his jaw. Then too, he had a loosey-goosey way of driving that was making me nervous. It looked to me like he was all over the road. From what I could gather, the VC had been spotted heading into a nearby village. That was just at dawn, and his patrol had "lit them up," as he put it. A few had gotten away into the village, but three had been killed, including a VC officer. The Troops back at the small compound we had left were busy gearing up to surround the village and evacuate all of its inhabitants to a New Life hamlet later in the morning. But the truth was, the Americans were fed up with the villagers and the trouble that originated from there. They emptied the *ville* and burned it to the ground by 1300 hours that day.

We came around a curve and a little ways down the road I could see a knot of heavily armed American troops standing around what looked like bundles of muddy black clothing.

The Buck Sergeant said, "Watch this!" He swerved the jeep towards the group of Americans, who scattered as he approached. *Ba-da-boomp bang, Ba-da-boomp bang, Ba-da-boomp bang!* The tires of the jeep and trailer thumped as we bounced over the bodies of the dead Viet Cong.

"Haw haw!" The Sergeant cried as he stomped the brake peddle and skidded to a halt in a cloud of dust.

The Lieutenant gave him a disgusted look. "Now why'n hell'd you go and do that Sergeant?"

"They don't care no more sir." Came the simple reply.

"What an asshole" I thought. It was obvious to me that he did it to get a reaction from me, the *Fucking New Guy.* I could see he was smirking at me.

The three Vietnamese had been dragged to the edge of the road and laid outside by side. They had been shot up pretty thoroughly and looked well dead. It made me a little queasy to look at them, but look I did; these were the first enemy I had seen. I noticed the jeep tires had left indents in their thighs. One, the so-called VC officer, had his lower jaw shot off. You could see his upper teeth and most of what had been his tongue, lying on his throat. His left leg below the knee was twisted at an unnatural angle, and there were little holes dappling his blood-smeared chest. His eyes were wide open.

"We got this pistol off of that gook Lieutenant there, and this map. You better look at it." One of the grunts handed a well used, well oiled and cared for American .45 and a folded piece of paper to the American Lieutenant.

The Lieutenant tried to make light of it. "Jeez, look at him. It's gonna take a first rate mortician to get him ready for the viewing."

"Yeah, we tried mouth-to-mouth, El Tee , but it was no use," another of the grunts snickered.

And so it went, one trooper trying to out-do the next with their attempts at gallows humor. At first, it sickened me, but I came to understand it was their protection from the grim knowledge that it could just as easily be them lying beside this road tomorrow morning. In fact, for most, if not all of these guys, it would be their turn to die in a few weeks. Their little circle of bunkers was overran the night of Tet 68. The map they found on the officer that morning was an extremely detailed scale drawing of our compound!

You know, it was the common belief that we were fighting a bunch of illiterate know-nothing farmers. But I myself had been a map maker in a small Civil Engineering firm just prior joining the army. I knew maps, and I could see an accomplished draftsman had drawn this one. The hand lettering on it was really good. Farmers, my ass!

Christmas, Fire Support Base Keene

The Huey landed and out jumped Old Saint Nicholas (actually one of the Top Sergeants over at the TOC) and two gorgeous mini-skirt clad round-eyes. Real girls from back in *The World!* Their hairstyles, pale skin and white go-go boots, reminded us of the far away and yet so familiar place they came from, the place we'd all come from. The word spread before them that these "helpers" had posed nude for some girly magazine or another back Stateside. As the trio spread their cheer along the bunker line, cat-calls came floating in from all over. The girls did a good job of ignoring the more ribald comments, probably old hat to them by now, and Santa gave his evil-eyed Top Sergeants stare to any troop who even looked as if he might get out of line and so much as touch one of them.

The catcalls came from everywhere, "Where you from girl?"

"You from Philly? I am!"

"Hey, I'm a lover! Make you a believer, baby!"

"Oh baby girrrll! I love you too much!"

"We go short time, two dolla! You can pay me next month, honey!"

"Just once damn it…just once," came a muttered oath near me.

Although he was up-staged by the female company, Santa was doing his part, helping the men forget the war, if only for a few moments. He was dressed in the traditional red suit, white beard, black boots and wide belt. In fact, with one jarring exception, he was done up right. The only real difference between him and any department store Santa back in *The World* was the .38 pistol strapped around his big pillow belly and the muzzle of the M-16 poking out of the huge gift bag strung over his shoulder. This Santa was serious.

A day or so later, we received some presents sent in the Christmas Spirit by some church group back in the states, some Christians intent on sending presents to the troops serving so far away from home; and bless their souls for having done so, it made a difference in ways they never knew. That day, this thoughtful group's donations to our morale was being handed out by the brigade Sergeant-Major as he stood at the head of the chow line; bless him too. Inside the bags were varieties of candies, paperback books, soap, shampoo and various other sundries—and dolls!

That's right, dolls! Honest, I couldn't make that up! Before long, you saw the dolls all over the place, pressed into the muddy path on the way to the piss tubes, or here and there, posed in some suggestive position on top of a bunker. One bunker was festooned with a grim little row of doll heads with their eyes burnt out. I remember I set mine on top of my bunker with a cigarette in its mouth. *Tough little doll*, I thought, and it amused me. Those damned things were everywhere, and you had to smile when you saw what the guys had done with them!

Beyond that, the troops loved the presents and the thought behind the gifts. One thing that they really took to was the brightly colored bags that had contained the goodies. These sturdy little canvas bags came in florescent red and florescent green, and for weeks afterward you could see columns of troops going out on sweeps with those bright red and green bags dangling off of their rucksacks. Long after the subdued color of their uniforms and gear faded into the distance you could follow their progress by watching the bright little bags bob over the landscape.

Of course, that may have been great for morale, but it wasn't doing much for the war effort, and eventually an order came down from On High to "Get rid of the damned things!" The brigade commander came out with that command because he'd figured out the bags were revealing troop movements. After all, he himself could plainly see them from his Command

Chopper as he flew around and micro-directed operations at 3000 feet AGL. He could only imagine what they looked like to the enemy.

A Story About John

I would see him here and there on various fire bases and at odd intervals. He would suddenly show up at my PURD site, usually unannounced because his company happened to be deployed to that particular operation. He always found me, not the other way around. He probably was attracted to the distinctive diamond shaped antenna on our PRD-1, which stuck out like a sore thumb.

John was 11th Bravo Infantry, a draftee sucked into this war from somewhere in Eastern Tennessee after a failing semester at college. He was a nice guy who went back to America in a government-issued casket. I wish I could remember his last name and the town he was from. Its always just on the tip of my tongue, but I have forgotten or blocked the information. I feel sad that I can't remember those things because back then we had long talks about everything under the sun…you know-girls and cars and *everything*-in a natural flowing discourse.

John and I seemed to just know each other right from the get-go. He had our mission nailed, too. He knew exactly what I and my partner were doing.

"You're listening to the VC aren't you!" he'd say.

"No, John," I'd reply, "I'm working Radio Relay, just passing on information."

There was no way could I admit the truth to him, even though I would have liked to. He was always cool with my answer though, but he knew better, he knew what I was really up to. But he didn't push it and so we developed a sort of mutual respect. When he'd show up, I'd greet him and we'd walk away from the Purd site so he couldn't hear the ditty bops, see our code pads or watch us work.

I would take a break. I was always glad for his company. We would rustle up some chow or walk over to his squad's area of the bunker line to talk and smoke for a while until, he'd be summoned to some duty by his squad or platoon leader. There was a never-ending round of work to be done by these infantrymen, bunkers to be built or reinforced, shit burning detail, weapons (both individual and squad) to be cleaned and inspected. The troopers and their gear were subjected to a continual round of inspections. They were kept on a short rein and were constantly gearing up for the unavoidable next sweep.

If I had it, I would bring along booze or beer to share with the guys in John's squad. In return they would inevitably offer me some of their most excellent dope. It was fine-cut, aromatic green stuff that promised a good high. They said they took off of the VC they killed (yes, the VC were dopers too).

He had a hard life. There was an air of sadness, tiredness and resignation in John, only leavened by his natural good nature. He accepted his lot, and had a ready smile whenever I saw him. He always came with a joke. I thought of him as intelligent, quick, and, in a strange way, *happy!*

I often wondered how he maintained his attitude, given his situation? I never could figure that one out. To me it seemed John was just trying to get through each day alive and whole, do his duty and get the hell out. He didn't care for the war, and given what his experience had been, and the things he had seen, didn't believe we were winning anything.

"We're just pissing one hell of a lot of people off," John would say.

His days and nights had to be far worse than anything I ever experienced in Vietnam. He told me stories of booby traps he'd avoided and of the time he'd survived an ambush because of dumb luck—he tripped and fell just as the ambush was sprung. Another time, his rucksack was pierced by a round from an AK-47, killing a can of Chopped Ham and Eggs.

"Damn," he'd say with a rueful grin, "that Chopped Ham & Eggs was my favorite."

I was glad I wasn't walking in his boots, and yet I had to admire his bravery, the casual way he had of doing what he did. Picture yourself standing up and walking slowly across a few hundred yards of open paddy land, knowing you could be dead in the next second. Now string a lot of seconds together, the time that it takes you to get across that open paddy. And now repeat it, day after grueling day. If these grunts got four hours of rest a night, let alone sleep, they counted themselves lucky. They did 45 to 60 days in the field, followed by three days of relative peace at base camp for rest and re-supply, a "Stand Down" as it was known.

That was the same schedule my partner and I had, but it was not at all the same for us. Their "field" time was filled with endless sweat-soaked sweeps, guard duty, outpost duty, and ambush patrols. More danger than I will ever know.

Once John showed up with his right foot bandaged. He managed to sport a big smile as he explained that because of his wound, he was released from humping the bush for a few days. It was odd, how he got that wound. One evening a member of his company had gone ape-shit, insanely raving to be sent home. The mentally disturbed trooper took a Vietnamese family hostage in their hooch. He dared anyone to come in and get him.

John and his squad surrounded the hooch, and then John approached the front door and attempted to talk the guy into surrendering. John thought he would be okay as they had been friends, but he received an M-16 round in the foot for his trouble. And then the guy shot himself. John just shook his head and smiled a sad smile.

Some time later, during a Stand Down, I was over at the Brigade's EM Club, a place we called The Long Branch Saloon. I recognized a member of John's squad, and asked about my friend.

"Yeah," the guy said, looking into his beer, "he was greased up near Tay Ninh."

"What? But…"

"He was walking point, I think." The guy shrugged, as if there wasn't anything else to say. Shit, what could you say? I couldn't think of anything.

Bait

It was north of Tay Ninh, on a small artillery training base manned by five Special Forces advisors, a small cadre of ARVN trainers, and about 150 of their highly suspected trainees. The tunnel was concrete lined and sloped down into a deep underground bunker that had been originally built by the French.

Normally, only the Special Forces were allowed in this bunker at night, but due to an alert, my partner and I had been invited to sleep there. We soon found out that the invitation had been extended with more than just our own well-being in mind. A lone wire mesh covered light bulb burned brightly a few feet inside the tunnels entrance, perhaps 50 feet away from where we waited. I personally was waiting for anything, ANYTHING, to enter that pool of light, if that happened I was ready to throw a grenade toward the light and follow it immediately with a twenty pellet "00 buck" shotgun round from my grenade launcher. Next, I would pick up the M-16 leaning against the sandbagged wall behind me, and the moment the grenade exploded, spray a magazine down the tunnel. That's pretty much as far as my planning had progressed. I didn't have any experience in these matters and it had taken me a while to work out the sequence. I was scared spitless. I could hear firing up top, but as of yet it didn't seem like anything of major consequence.

A sandy haired, gin breathed Special Forces Staff Sergeant had posted me at this end of the tunnel as a guard, but I felt I was more like a living "trip-wire." It was patently plain to me that I would be the first to go if anything happened. So you can see I was none too happy about the whole thing. The Sergeant's instructions were both direct and simple.

"Shoot anyone who enters the tunnel," he said. "And I mean anyone!"

"Even the ARVN?" I had asked, already knowing the answer.

"Particularly the ARVN, they know better than to come in here at night or during an alert!"

"You want me to shoot the ARVN." I couldn't digest this. "What about Lieutenant Vinh?"

"Especially that prick! Kill him and I'll get you a Bronze Star and a trip to Vung Tau! Can't prove it but we think he's a fucking VC. Hell, we don't know who is and who isn't a VC around here. Sometimes we think we're running a goddamned VC R&R slash Training Center!"

I had a sinking feeling as I realized the gravity of our situation. We had been running our classified PRD-1 operation and sleeping near the trainee's area for almost a week now, and here they were, using us for bait for the VC!

I guarded the tunnel for several long hours after that. Fortunately, no one tried to enter. Eventually the firing settled down, and the SF's radios stopped chattering. The next morning my partner Carpenter and I had a long radio conversation with our detachment's commander back at Long Binh and, with his permission, got the hell out of there before nightfall.

Turtle Base Mystery

This happened at Fire Support Base Turtle, near Long Binh, soon after Tet 68. The mission here was to prevent the VC from blowing up the Long Binh ammo dump. Unfortunately, they did blow it up, anyway.

I had come out of a deep sleep and had risen to a sitting position. I was still in that twilight state between sleep and waking. It dawned on me that I had slipped off to never-never land a couple of hours before while I was supposed to be manning the PRD-1. I stood up and stepped over the sandbag wall surrounding the PRD-1 site, intending go and fill my steel pot with water for coffee and a whore's bath. As I did so, I glanced down the slope some distance to where four Brothers were warming themselves at a fire built inside a 30 gallon oil drum. I had noticed them doing this for several mornings now; all I could do was wonder why they did it in the heat. CRACK! Almost at the moment my gaze alighted on them, the drum violently exploded, flinging all but one of them back and down except for the one nearest me who was blown upwards.

I only saw the beginning of his arc. As I dove backwards over the sand-bag wall, his scream followed me in.

What the hell was that, a single explosion and then nothing? A lucky shot with a mortar? Not likely. Nothing made sense. *RPG?* Naw, I hadn't heard it fire or roar in. I figured it maybe was a grenade. When I looked again there were troopers running toward the victims and cries of "Medic" were going up from several locations. The brother who had been airborne moments before was now holding his crotch and moaning as he rolled downhill. Another was trying to stand up and the other two were just lying there. I stayed put, as there seemed to be plenty of help forming around those who needed it. I watched the medics at work in the middle of the crowd that formed, and saw stretchers were brought over. Soon a Medivac chopper was rising through the red clay dust to ferry the wounded troopers to the next echelon of care. By now I had a pretty good idea of what had happened. During the night someone had booby-trapped the barrel, and it sure as hell hadn't been the NVA!

FSB Turtle Memories

"Blazer One Zero this is Two-Two…Ruddy, you there?…Ruddy, key your mike if you can't talk. Over!"

I was breaking radio procedure by using Ruddy's nickname, but I did-n't give a hot shit. Sappers had once again managed to blow up the Long Binh ammo dump, and Ruddy's PRD-1 team was sited on that base. A few moments ago I had been twirling the antenna on my PRD-1 when a blinding flash lit the night sky like it was daylight. I could actually feel the heat on the back of my neck.

My immediate reaction was to dive to the bottom of the bunker. But there was no noise. Practically before I had time to think *That's weird!,* the flash was followed by a deep resounding blast and rumble! I looked over the lip of the bunker and saw a tremendous explosion in progress. It looked like a nuclear detonation, complete with a gigantic mushroom cloud. Secondary explosions lit the underside of the mushroom cloud as a variety of ordinance including White Phosphorus rounds cart-wheeled through the air. It had taken a few seconds for the shock waves to travel the mile or so separating FSB Turtle from the ammo dump.

SP5 Ruddy Reynolds was a great guy and a friend. He was also one of the funniest men I had ever known. Give him a couple of beers and he would go into his South Carolina Baptist Preacher imitation and have you rolling on the floor for half the night. I couldn't stand the thought of Ruddy and his partner dying in that mess over there. My guts were twisted in knots as I tried to contact him.

"Blazer One Zero, Two-Two. Over" I shouted into my radio. "Blazer One Zero, this is Two-Two. Come in. Over" Still no answer. "Blazer One Zero, this is Two-Two…Ruddy, key your mike if you can't talk. Over."

I had visions of Ruddy hearing me but being too wounded to respond verbally to my transmissions. Or maybe he was surrounded. Why else was he not responding? Still nothing…It had been several minutes now and other teams on the DF net were beginning to call me, wanting to know what was going on, including "Six Actual" our commander back at the Det on Long Binh.

I reported what little I could see and asked that the net remain clear so that I'd have a chance of hearing any answering transmission from the team. I figured I had the best chance since I was closest to them.

While calling every ten seconds or so, I watched as two helicopters glided over the base. Suddenly there was a second huge explosion and the choppers were engulfed—they just disappeared!

I renewed my efforts, "Blazer One-Zero, Blazer Two-Two. Answer! Over."

"Two-Two, this is One-Zero, we're alright, we're alright!" A quavering voice finally came out of my radio's speaker. It was Ruddy, sounding out of breath and scared.

"One-Zero, Two-Two, damn boy, you 'bout scared us to death, how are you guys? Over."

"My worthless NUG is still back in our sleeping bunker, Two-Two, he's too scared to stand up just yet. Boy, you ought to see his face though! I'm all right, just deaf and blind, can't see anything here, too much dust, that's why it took so long to answer. That first one blew the PURD bunker flat and knocked the jeep twenty feet and over on its side, the only way I could locate it was by crawling towards the sound of your voice. When I got close enough I could see the red light flash every time you transmitted."

God, was I happy to hear his voice! After he signed off, he and his partner righted their jeep and the next day they drove over to our site (hardy little beasts, those Jeeps!).

Ruddy told us that what had almost certainly saved them from injury was his having to go to the teams sleeping bunker to wake up the sleepyhead new guy, who should have relieved him at the PRD-1 site earlier.

But then it was typical Ruddy, almost in his next breath he was flip'n me shit over how worried I had sounded when I was trying to raise him. He said he couldn't help laughing as he crawled toward "Mother Parks" frantic calls.

His voice took a more sober tone as he told us too of the fate of those in the two choppers. The crews, and members of an MP combat reaction force they were delivering, had all had been killed, actually pretty much vaporized. The total was over twenty dead, gone in an instant, just like that.

Near the "French Plantation" in the Iron Triangle

Our brigade was in support of the Big Red One, the 1st Infantry Division. The radio had sparked the welcome message about fifteen minutes previous; Sergeant-Major Parks, my dad, had showed up at the 856th's compound back at Long Binh earlier in the morning expecting to see his son.

Dad was serving with an Engineer outfit up at Pleiku and had taken a couple of days off to look me up. I was given permission to come in from the field and visit with him. *Fantastic!* And just when I needed a break, too! I gathered up my gear amid the comments of my comrades concerning my privileges as an Army brat (as if!), and headed over toward the LZ.

I hadn't gone a hundred feet when the yell went up for everyone to stop where they were and stand in place; mines had been found. We had only been here since early last evening, having convoyed in and set up operations in a bombed out plantation during the last hours of daylight.

I immediately came to a screeching halt and broke a sweat. I didn't like the idea of mines, they gave me the willies. As I stood there, I wondered that no one had been killed since last evening when we had occupied this little patch of Vietnam! Ten minutes turned into an hour as I stood there. Anyone who was fool enough to move was yelled at and told to stop screwing around. A chopper came in and landed on the road some distance from me and out hopped several troopers festooned with mine detecting gear. One two-man team began sweeping toward the TOC, while another swept down the bunker line.

As the sweepers made their way over the ground, every once in a while they would plant a little flag to mark the location of a mine. As they swept, they would trail out white plastic tape to define the cleared areas. There weren't many little flags so far, though. After sweeping the TOC area they swept down to the chopper pad and then began sweeping toward individuals.

An hour turned into two, and then two and a half. By now I was near heat stroke, standing there under the sun. My helmet, flak jacket, and web-gear, weapon, and two Claymore bags full of M-79 rounds, felt like they added up to at least a ton of dead weight. I figured if the sweepers didn't get to me soon all they would find was a grease spot under all this crap.

Finally a team swept up to me. As they reached me I asked them what they were finding.

"Bouncing Betty's", came the professional reply. "Been here since the French war, judging by their condition. Stay inside the tape, go slow and keep your eye's open."

Bouncing Betty? What in the hell was that? I wondered.

My dad was standing in the door of the 856th's barracks when I hopped out of the jeep that brought me from Redcatcher pad. My appearance seemed to shock the good sergeant, and I knew why. In an effort to spare my mother worry I had never revealed to either of my parents that I spent my time in the field. For all either of them knew I was living in relative safety, spending my tour at our detachments HQ on Long Binh. My stained jungle fatigues, boots with all the black scuffed off of them, and the gear, told a different story. And of course, I probably looked all the worse for what I had just gone through.

Several hours later we were sitting in a little bar in downtown Saigon, drinking beer, fending off the bar girls and trading stories. In fact, we were having a pretty good visit. He told me how the ARVN, in treacherous league with the Viet Cong, had shelled his base with 105's; and another story about the VC sappers, greased from head to toe and totally nude, that had infiltrated his compound the night of Tet. Keeping my end of the conversation up, I told him my Tet story of the three VC Sappers who had been found dead, three days after the assault, floating in the water tower that supplied our water at Bien Hoa airbase.

We avoided the subject of what I really did in Vietnam. He knew it was classified and he left it alone. But he did extract from me the fact that

I was in the field. I tried to assure him that I was mostly on Fire Support Bases and that it wasn't too bad, and we let it go at that.

He told a tale of how his dog had wandered into the mine field surrounding his compound in Pleiku and had managed to blow itself up. I took the opportunity to ask him what a Bouncing Betty was.

"Oh, those damned things! Germans used those in World War Two, my company walked into a field full of them outside a village in northern France in '44! We lost six guys before we knew they were there. When you step on one, it arms itself, when your foot comes off of it, it jumps up about waist high and explodes. Full of ball bearings. Nasty SOB's, damned Krauts. Why do you ask, Dave?"

"Just wondering, that's all, heard some guys talking about them. Have you heard from Mother lately?"

FSB Keene, Mid-December, 67

It was time to obtain a new COMUS pad, and toward that end I had walked over to the chopper pad to hitch a ride back to Redcatcher. Sitting on the pad was one of those little two seat "bubble" choppers that looked like nothing so much as an overgrown insect, you know, the ones with the wire-frame tail booms. A spiffily dressed Major was walking toward it. He had on spit-shined boots and fatigues pressed to the nines. He had a folding stock AK hanging from his shoulder that was sporting three 30 round magazines taped together. I had never seen one rigged like that.

"Where you headed, Specialist?" He cheerfully asked, even before I had a chance to speak.

"Redcatcher pad, Sir" I replied.

"Good, I need someone to ride shotgun, hop in."

The Major did a quick pre-flight on the little chopper and briskly climbed in. He was obviously enjoying the hell out of himself. Heck, so was I! I had never flown in one of these eggbeaters before and was looking forward to the experience.

The Major fired up the chopper's engine (It was a loud sucker), flicked a bunch of toggle switches and fiddled with the radio knobs. I noticed the bubble was filled with the smell of English Leather aftershave lotion and burnt aviation fuel. He handed me a pilot's helmet and showed me how to key the intercom. I fiddled with the unfamiliar seat-belt and harness rig and played with the visor on the ill-fitting helmet, finally settling on leaving it up. *Neat stuff!*

"Stow that gear and strap in; we're fly'n low level all the way back, Specialist" said the good Major as he revved the engine and worked the controls. I nodded once and we smoothly lifted off. We had gained maybe a hundred feet or so and had just cleared the bunker line when the ships nose abruptly tilted down and the ground came rushing up, I put the brakes on with both feet! The maneuver was so unexpected that I had involuntarily stiffened my feet against the control peddles on my side to the chopper.

"Take your feet off of the peddles, damn it!" The shout came over my headset. I did as I was told while simultaneously removing my embedded fingernails from the stock of my weapon. The Major recovered and leveled the ship just off the deck. He gunned the engine and sped forward.

"No need for that now, Specialist; I'll do the flying; you keep a look-out for Mr. Charles!"

The tree line several hundred yards out from the bunker line rapidly loomed dead ahead! We, on the other hand, were still on the deck, skimming just over the top of the scrub brush that seemed to be rushing by mere inches beneath the skids. The solid wall of jungle had just filled the windshield when the Major jerked his arm up and the little ship shot seemingly straight up at a cock-eyed angle! The engine sounded like it was tearing itself off its mounts as we popped up over the trees and then dropped down in among the tops of them.

My stomach was somewhere back there at the edge of the jungle. The Major looked over at me and smiled.

Real funny, I thought, embarrassed because I knew my face revealed how frightened I was. The grinning loon was now flying just above, no, among the tree tops, tipping the chopper first one way and then another and sliding it all over the place. I would barely have time to brace for one crash when the son-of-a-bitch would zip around an obstacle and point the ship at a fresh new seeming-disaster. It was all just so damned FAST! I had a death grip on the seat beneath me. And just when I was getting used to the treetop flying (not really), we suddenly shot out over a clearing and into another death-defying dive. I managed to not brace against the pedals this time but that was only because I was preoccupied with not allowing the seat cushion to be sucked up my arse. I shouldn't have worried though, as I was frozen in place and we were now in freefall.

Surrendering to the Major's flying genius, I closed my eyes and tried to remember how to breath and to calculate how long it would take us to reach Redcatcher pad. But it was no use, my cognitive faculties were frozen, too. In vain, I tried to convince myself that everything would be all right and that I would be back on the ground soon enough. But that did not help either, every second seemed like an hour. Hell, if he'd let me out, I'd gladly have walked back to Long Binh. But that was not an option as we weren't talking, I hated him. We crossed the clearing and zoomed up the wall of trees as before, and soon enough were again weaving among the tree tops.

I was having a delicious fantasy of how, if I survived the crash and the VC, I would murder the Major and make it look as if he had died in the crash. *Beg, motherfucker!* I would say before I shot him with his own AK-47. We were coming over the edge of yet another clearing and I was anticipating the inevitable suicide dive when the ship was instantly wrenched vertically on its side, my side! I now found myself looking over my right shoulder at the ground, right there! Before I could scream, the bucket of bolts was just as suddenly leveled and we shot off at an angle from our original course and back over the trees.

"Got to keep 'em guessing!" Major Asshole said, almost to himself.

"Who, me?" I asked weakly, the first words I had spoken since taking off. I wasn't in the mood for conversation as I could feel the bile rising in my throat.

"Noooo, didn't you see those "farmers" at the far edge of that clearing?"

"Hell no…huh, sir"

"Wanna go back and see them?"

"HELL NO, SIR!"

It was a blessed sight to see Long Binh loom out of the ground haze. The Major made a snappy approach and put the chopper down near a fueling station. He shut down and jumped out, strolling over to one of the enlisted types manning the depot. I climbed out, barely managing not to puke, and made my way directly to the waiting jeep for my ride to the Det. Maybe it was impolite, but I didn't bother to go over and thank the Major for the ride.

Fishnet Factory, on the outskirts of Saigon, Late 1968

The Buck Sergeant's face was flushed with effort and contorted with rage. He had lured the children in range by tossing candy and C-rations to them. Now he was hurling C-rat cans AT them as hard as he could.

"Take THAT you muthafuckas,!" he yelled as he fired a can at one of the kids from the roof of the two story building, part of the complex we knew as the Fishnet Factory.

Undaunted, taking turns, the grinning kids continued to dash in and extricate the cans from the sticky mud of the rice paddy while their buddies kept a close watch on the roof.

"Stop the shit, Carl, you're gonna hurt one of those lil' pukes," a member of the Sergeant's squad said as he flipped his tattered cards over in a perpetual game of solitaire.

"Goddamned good idea," Carl returned as he pulled a beehive round out of its cardboard canister and began to take the poncho covering off of the 90mm recoilless rifle.

That's when he was jumped, wrestled to the deck, and sat on by several troopers. Raving to be let free, he struggled with all his strength, and it was plain to see that he was very much out of control. The platoon leader was summoned and eventually Carl's weeping figure was lead off down the stairs. A little while later he was seen boarding a chopper in the care of the platoon's medic.

"I knew there was something up with that fucker when he charged that machine gun last week," one of his troops said as we watched Carl board the chopper. The Sergeant had been recommended for a Bronze Star for that act of bravery, but charging into the face of death can have some nasty side effects.

On A Road Coming Out Of Saigon

The little bastards were quick, you had to give them that. And they were persistent, too. They had already been shooed away several times. Our jeep was slowed by the traffic ahead and that's when one swooped in and snatched the carton of Marlboro's out of the back. But equally quick was the Specialist Fifth Class who leaped out of the passenger side of the jeep, taking his M-16 with him.

"Give 'em back you little cocksuckers!", he yelled at the top of his lungs.

The kids had retreated a few steps. Now they half turned, prepared to run. They looked back, their eyes intent on the American.

"God-damnit! I want those fucking cigarettes back, NOW!" He pointed the M-16 at them. The kids stood their ground, not looking afraid, just alert. One, at the back of the pack, took off running with the carton of cigarettes that had been hidden behind his back until now.

"OK, you little bastard!" The Spec 5 shouted, releasing the safety on his M-16. At that moment the Specialist was distracted by several ARVN soldiers who had stepped out on the third floor balcony of an apartment complex a little ways off. Some were armed, and all were looking his way, talking excitedly.

That Specialist 5th Class was me. I got back into the jeep and my partner sped off. I was badly shaken, for I knew in my heart that I had fully intended to shoot those kids. After ten months in country, something had surely changed in me.

The Fishnet Factory Again

Hummmm…Little Needle Dick…I've often wondered what become of the little bugger! And what of his parents? He's a grown man now, way older than we were then. His parents, if they survived, would be about my age now. He was, when I knew him, a little boy of two and a half or maybe three, with bright black eyes charged with a sort of smiling inquisitive innocence that was always in motion. *A neat kid,* we all thought. Some grunt-wag named him "Needle Dick, The Bug Fucker" because he was never seen in anything but an ill-fitting T-shirt and his tiny little tally whacker was always "blowing in the breeze."

Needle Dick's parents were the caretakers of the Fishnet Factory and I suppose that his dad had once worked there when it actually was still in operation, making fishnets for the Vietnamese fishing fleet. I and my RRD cohorts bunked in the room next to the quarters where Needle Dick's family lived.

One afternoon, Needle Dick was visiting us as he often did. He was scarfing up, as usual, all the C-ration peanut butter and pound cake we could feed him when his dad knocked at our doorsill and bowed. He said something low in Vietnamese. We responded with bows and smiles of our own and invited him in. Although we had difficulty communicating, he used hand gestures and we understood that it was time for the boy to come home and eat. Naturally, that was okay with us, but first why didn't dad have a beer with us? He readily agreed and gratefully accepted the cold Budweiser. As we drank we proceeded to sign to one another, touching on topics both simple and confused. I didn't have a clue what he was saying, and I don't think he knew what I was saying, either. However, this wasn't a problem. Pretty soon someone broke out the whiskey and the bottle went its rounds. After a few snorts, Needle Dick's dad was visibly looped! He didn't stop there though, and soon enough he was a jolly old soul. There is nothing like Boiler Makers to oil up a conversation and lower the language barrier.

And it was about there when Needle Dick's mom showed up, looking for the both of them. If looks could kill, we American gangsters would have died then and there from the look she gave us! Of course, one look was all it took for her to recognize the condition her spouse was in.

Hubby suddenly sobered as she turned her attention on him and fired off a high-pitched volley of rapid Vietnamese. But the booze was on him and he seemed to think he could handle her. That was a big mistake. It wasn't too hard to follow the substance of what passed between them, and it was easy enough to see who the victor was. She gave papa-san a tongue lashing to beat the band, and, snatching up smiling little peanut butter-smeared Needle Dick, she disappeared.

A man should be aware of his limitations, and it was embarrassingly obvious that papa-san had just found one of his. You know, those Viets were not all that different from us after all.

Being a Vietnamese linguist with a Top Secret Codeword clearance could give a person an insight into some facets of the Southeast Asian conflict that you might not see anywhere else. Was it mentioned earlier that military intelligence spooks and spies tend to be idealistic and even hopeless romantics? Perhaps that is because it would be nearly impossible to find anyone else who might want the job.

DO NOT DISTURB THE GHOST

By John Klawitter

"Women are trouble, anyway," Harvey reflected, with that knowing hint of old Jewish wisdom rising in his voice. "But when they're already crying before you meet them-that's *real* trouble."

Harvey Goldfine and I were walking along the tarmac at the side of the Tan Son Nhut Airport runway. He was a Spec 4, and I'd just been awarded the first curved stripe over my own golden eagle. We were headed from Davis Station to a stout cinderblock bungalow called the White Shack, where I ran a small section that attempted to decrypt and translate low level Viet Cong intercept. Small section was right. At the time, I had Goldfine and Raymer, and that was about it.

This was in February of 1965, the *dry time*, and so the weather was actually pleasant, not too tepid and sometimes even a little breeze to blow the smog haze that came from a million Saigon charcoal burners out over the South China Sea. It was late morning and the flapping Hueys were long gone from Tan Son Nhut. Air traffic was light, just an occasional war bird lifting off to rejoin its fellows on a carrier somewhere or taking a special order run to drop a little napalm somewhere in the jungle.

Harvey and I were on the noon-to-eight shift. Having a little time to kill, we stopped off for a spot of refreshment at a small U.S. army-built processing station with a restaurant that featured milk shakes and massive air conditioning. The woman who had moved Harvey to comment on the disaster associated with the typical man-woman relationship was barely more than a girl, at least that's the way she seemed to me at first glance. She cried softly to herself while she took our order, and then stood over the shake blenders, her shoulders slumped in her grief while she spooned in chocolate syrup.

"On the other hand," Harvey said, flicking an imaginary cigar in his best Groucho Marx imitation, "A set of knockers the size of hers, I haven't seen this side of Honolulu." There was no question about it. She had a large and full figure while your average Vietnamese ladies tended towards lithe and willowy. Chinese, maybe, I was thinking to myself. But Harvey was already in action.

"*Co…,*" he said, raising his voice, "*Co manh gioi, khong?*" Harvey never lacked for balls, but his Vietnamese wasn't all that great. Like me, he was better pouring through Hoa's Viet-English dictionary than actually conversing in the field. I knew that in saying hello he'd just about maxed out his linguistic skills. But it didn't matter. She responded to his question with a rising wail and rushed into a back room, leaving the blenders unattended. A glum middle-aged *Ba* had to finish the job but the blenders had run so long the milkshakes were warm and soupy.

"She's all yours, Kha," Harvey shrugged, rejecting his overdone drink with a disgusted wave of his hand. In Vietnam, the little things from home, like actually being able to melt the tiny crystals of ice cream on your tongue, meant more than one might imagine *back in the temperate zone*.

"Meet you at the Shack," he said. With that, he replaced his stovepipe hat and gave me a little farewell wave. In another moment he'd wandered out the door and was sauntering down the runway. The thought struck me that this was going to be an epic day; Goldfine was actually going to get to work before I did.

I cracked open the twin books I was carrying and took a formed plastic seat at one of the formica tables. At that time I was in the heart of my Francophile phase; I was taking a course downtown at L'Ecole Francaise and was slowly churning my way through Camus's La Peste with paperback copies in both English and French. I sat at one of the Formica tables and slowly moved my six-inch ruler down the page. It was the season of the wet in Oran, a large French Port on the Algerian coast; rats were bleeding in the streets and things in general were starting to go sour for the citizens, who saw the riders of the apocalypse approaching but had nowhere to go. That was appropriate imagery for South Vietnam in 1965.

After a while the girl returned from the back room. I watched her daub at her eyes with a tissue. They were large and soft eyes, and I thought her extraordinarily lovely, even in this city of beautiful women. And then, to my wondering surprise, she came from behind the counter and started to come over to my table. I smiled, hoping I was projecting encouragement rather than admiration for her breasts.

The old Ba behind her gave a sharp hawking sound, something like a throat-clearing grunt of warning, but the girl ignored her. She came closer and then sat daintily across the table from me.

"I did not-" she began in halting English. "I did not mean to scorn your friend."

"No, It's alright," I said.

Her tears started again, and it was a moment before she could speak.

"Forgive me. I have had some very bad luck," she said. "Bad things have happened to me."

Her hand moved across the table and brushed against my own, just for a moment. When it came to the opposite sex, I was both blessed and cursed with an extraordinary imagination; that touch reminded me of the soft feathers of a small bird's wing. I wished she'd touch me like that again. Or perhaps her hand might even linger, pausing in some existentially satisfactory way with light pressure against my own. You see, I was recently out of college where I'd spend my days with my nose stuck in books of literature, poetry and languid prose, entire volumes wherein male and female lingered over flowery passages of verse before they rushed off to do the mad dance of pressed flesh. I still believed that was the way one did it.

My reverie was interrupted by an argument coming from the back room. The old *ba* was talking to someone in loud and disapproving tones. After a moment, I saw it was an ARVN air force lieutenant. He was a lightweight, probably topping the scale at 110. But his moustache, worn Nguyen Cao Ky style, was bristling. His arms were crossed, and his lips were clamped shut in a tight line. He and the old *ba* stared silently at our table.

The girl broke under the pressure of their furious glances and jumped up from the table. But then, wonder of wonders, there was a soft touch on my arm, this time a light caress.

"Meet me here tomorrow morning at this time," she whispered.

"What's your name?"

"Nhut," she said. "Co Nhut. And yours?"

"Jack"

"Jack," she repeated with a wan smile. She pronounced it *Zac*. "*Giac co den.*" And then she gave the disapproving couple a defiant look and retreated behind the counter.

I practically ran to my gunmetal gray desk at the White Shack, where I eagerly reached for my Hoa's. *Giac co den* meant "Jack Black Flag," the Vietnamese expression for *pirate*. I smiled, thinking I was some sort of pirate lover in her innocent world. As the afternoon of dull and boring transcriptions wore on (SAW TWO INVADER GANGSTER AMERI-CANS YESTERDAY...BONG NEED MORE RICE...SEND MORE BULLETS RIGHT AWAY...ONE NGUOI MY PIG CAUGHT ON PUNJI STAKE...), I'm afraid my imagination ran with the Co Nhut thing. I was Jack The Pirate Lover, swooping down from my brigantine frigate to carry the pretty and vulnerable Nhut away to my love nest and shower her with doubloons and ruby necklaces and fancy silks.

The next morning I showed up a half hour early for my milkshake, and that pleased her. The old *ba* and the little ARVN flyboy were nowhere around. It's not that I was worried about him. The Americans in our unit tended to look down on ARVN officers. The arvins, as they were commonly called, *worked for us.* I tried to be polite about it, but I had the same common perception as everybody else. *If they wanted to win so damn bad, why were they standing back and letting us do the fighting?* Part of me knew that wasn't fair, and yet I'd seen so much corruption by that time that I figured a G.I. enlisted man's stripes were worth more than all the tarnished 3rd World Country stars and bars in the whole damn country.

Co Nhut apparently didn't have any problems with his not being there, either, because she came right over to my table and sat down. Her eyes were puffy and she looked like she'd spent the night crying.

"I see you are a person of education." She indicated the twin copies of La Peste at my side. "This is good. I need your scholarly help very badly."

"Anything," I declared valiantly, "what is it?"

But I wasn't about to find out, because at that moment a group of four Vietnamese air force officers burst in the door and headed angrily for the back room. It was a full hand, three lieutenants and a captain. The Captain called angrily to her, indicating with a nod of the head that she was to follow. She jerked around like a kid caught eating a stolen candy bar.

"Tomorrow. Here." She hissed at me. "Seven in the morning. Can you make it?"

"Of course. I'll be here." Again I felt that delicious lingering brush of her hand on my arm, and this time a quick kiss on my cheek and then she was gone.

My day and the night that followed were filled with lusty pirate dreams. The next morning I ran naked through the morning fog from my barracks to the shower and back again. I dressed like I was on automatic pilot, enduring a few jeering mutters from Harvey, something about *The things a guy will do for a piece of ass,* as he rolled over under his triple mosquito netting and put his extra pillow over his head.

It was still half-light and pairs of Supersabers, F101s and A10s were thundering down the runway. Their tails glowed as they followed one another into the low fog, off to do a war somewhere. Swarms of olive-colored choppers rose and circled overhead and then flapped away, mostly headed north and west. An occasional dragon ship drifted in like a weary bee, returning from night vigil dropping flares and spraying lead around the perimeter of distant hamlets.

True to her word, Nhut was waiting inside the deserted restaurant. It was too early for a milkshake, so she got me a cup of coffee. We sat at the table with our heads close together and she poured out her heart to me.

"It is all about my brother," she said, slowing her Vietnamese down so I could catch the general drift, and repeating in halting English when she found I wasn't following.

"Your brother?" That surprised me, seeming as it did to come out of the blue.

"Yes, my older brother. I will explain. A few years ago, he—died in an unlucky airplane crash."

"I'm sorry…"

She shook her head impatiently. "Yes. But now the United States military—your people—want to dig up his body."

"No…why would they do that?"

"Yes! They say they want to confirm his death."

"I see…"

"No. You do *not* see. We—I am Buddhist. Such a desecration of the grave violates all that Buddha teaches. My brother's *ma,* his ghost, must not be disturbed. He must be allowed to rest in peace or he will wander as a lost one through all eternity."

I was stunned. It was outside my experience, but it didn't sound like something that a Christian nation would do. "There must be some mistake," I protested.

"No mistake, *Giac co den.* I ask you, What sort of barbarians would violate the sacred rights of the dead?"

"What can I do?"

"My English is not so good. You must talk to them for me."

"To who? Where?" I asked, startled at this new turn of events.

"Downtown," she said simply.

My mornings were free, so I figured it could be done. We agreed to meet the next morning at the Tan Son Nhut main gate and catch a cab together.

This would be something new for me. Sure, I'd learned my little crypto games at the Puzzle Palace and I had a green Top Secret badge with my picture on one side and thumb print on the other, but in truth my knowledge was highly specialized and I actually knew very little about the real war. I could tell you roughly where the Viet Cong cells were nestled like little cancers in the districts and provinces across South Vietnam, but I wouldn't know a VC if he came up and stuck a gun in my face.

Co Nhut showed up wearing the white ao dai and black pants of a schoolgirl. The only thing missing was the conical straw hat. If it wasn't for the knowing look in her eyes and that great body, she looked young enough to throw one leg over a bike and pedal off to the academy like any teenage schoolgirl.

"We go to my apartment first," she said simply. *Hot damn!* We drove off towards Cho Lon in silence, me with visions of sugarplums dancing in my head. The apartment was clean and bright. As we entered, a wrinkled old woman fixed me with a silent stare. *All these old ba ladies hanging around!* Nhut saw the old lady was bothering me. She let out a string of some sing-song language. Not Vietnamese, it had to be Chinese. Whatever, the old woman grunted once and left the room. A healthy two-year old girl remained, staring up at me from a seat on the sofa.

"The bedroom is there," Nhut said simply, pointing to another door.

First it had been the presence of the old ba, and now there was this child…I know it was crazy, but with the kid staring at me, the idea of sex blew out of my mind like I didn't know what it was.

"Let's talk about what we have to do," I said.

Nhut looked relieved, and that, in turn, took the pressure off me. You never know how a woman is going to react when you turn down a roll in the hay. We sat across from each other at a small kitchen table. I took out a few ball-point pens and a pad of paper.

"There is an evil woman from America involved," she said. Co Nhut's problems were evolving into something that was more and more complex. I was starting to feel like I was walking ankle-deep in warm and slippery butter.

"An evil woman…" I repeated. "What did this bad woman do?"

"I already told you," Nhut said. She sounded nettled, sorry she had confided in someone as stupid as I was. There is a vein of strong impatience in Vietnamese women. They call it *Su Tu Hao Gam*, from the old legend of the tigeress-women of Hao Gam, or more simply, the tiger-lady. Simply stated, an impatient Vietnamese woman can cut you with a glance.

"She wants to disturb the *ma* of my brother."

Our plan had been to hear her story and then go to the American authorities, but if she was going to spoon it out to me in little dribbles, I didn't know when I'd ever hear the whole thing.

"Why don't we just go over there and talk to them now?" I suggested.

Practically before the words were out of my mouth I realized that was a mistake. Her face brightened instantly, "You would do that for me?"

"Sure…," I said, somewhat less enthusiastically.

JAG-MACV was the legal arm of the U.S. military effort. If I remember correctly, at that time it was on the second floor of an ordinary-looking building on Le Loi Street. The people there were not pleased to see us. A pimply-faced clerk gave me a sour look as he shoved a sign-in clipboard in my direction.

"What are *you* doing here?" he asked with all the disdain an E-3 could muster.

"I'm with her."

"Oh, her," he said. He addressed Co Nhut directly for the first time, "Lady, do you have an appointment?"

"We no need appointment!" Co Nhut barked. Her voice went up a notch, and the E-3 retreated to a back-room office and returned with a full bird in tow.

"Hello, I'm Colonel Greene," the colonel said. He was maybe 55 years old, a tall professional-looking fellow with curly gray hair.

"Spec. 5 Klawitter, Sir."

I was in civvies and unsure of the protocol. He waved off my salute, "At ease, son. How'd you get involved in this?"

My heart sank. *Involved.* I was involved in something.

"Well, sir, I'm stationed out at Tan Son Nhut, and-"

"Unit?" He sure knew how to cut through the crap.

"3rd RRU, sir. ASA."

"Clearance?"

"Top Secret Codeword."

"Badge?"

I showed him the tip end of it. He held out his hand and I reluctantly passed my badge across. We were never supposed to wear our badge downtown, and never *never* supposed to hand it over to anybody. He gave it to the E-3, who immediately got on the phone, presumably to call my CO at the 3rd.

The colonel pointed to a chair next to a pile of ratty magazines.

"Sit over there. I'll talk to her first, and then to you."

"No," Co Nhut protested. "I want him come with me!"

"No. My office, my rules, Ba Minh."

He took her by the arm and led her into his office. *Ba Minh! Ba* meant she was married! I stood there with the confused thoughts whirling in my head. *What was going on?*

"Sit over there," the E-3 pointed to a folding chair. His voice said I was going to catch a pile of *merde*. I took a seat and started through a pile of well-worn magazines.

Newsweek said the kids at Michigan State were staging a protest against the war. That seemed oddly unpatriotic to me. I couldn't concentrate on the details. Ford had a new sportster called the Mustang. Lucky Strikes meant fine tobacco. Canadian Club was smooth as velvet. From behind the paneled wood walls, Co Nhut—that is, Ba Minh's—voice was rising in a shrill crescendo. I couldn't make out the words, but the Colonel's solid bass was right in there, counter-punching and undercutting her blow for blow.

After a time, the door opened and Ba Minh marched out looking angry and defiant. It could have been five or fifteen minutes; in my state of mind, it wouldn't have made any difference.

The Colonel's cheeks were flushed an angry crimson, an unhealthy contrast to his gray locks. He nodded to me with a gesture that I took as more weary than unfriendly, "Okay, Spec 5. Your turn."

His office was heavy with dark mahogany paneled walls, and there were volumes of maroon and green law books behind glass paneled sliding doors. I stood in my unease. He sat on the edge of his big wooden desk, fiddling with the chain on my badge.

"Ordinarily, I wouldn't say two hoots to you," he said. "But we checked out the clearance. As a top secret guy, I don't expect any of this will be news to you."

I felt a little shiver of anticipation. He was about to make the mistake people who weren't in the spy biz sometimes did, that clearances meant you knew a lot of Top Secret crap, when actually by their very nature they were narrow as possible, defined only by the phrase *Need to know.*

"I'm going to fill you in," he continued in his weary lawyerly tone. "In return, I hope you can talk some sense into your lady friend, who represents nothing but trouble for me."

"Okay. But what is all this about her dead brother and the grave and everything?"

"Husband. It's her husband," the Colonel said. "There is no brother."

I blew out a deep breath and sat down. It wasn't that I loved her or anything like that. I just felt like a sucker.

"Well then, what about the evil lady from America?"

The colonel gave me a clipped little laugh. "That's what she's calling her? That would be Mrs. Harris, the wife of Captain Harris, U.S. Army, now officially deceased."

He saw the puzzled look growing on my face. "Look, let me start further back. I have to tell you a story before any of this will make sense. Let's just say there's an unofficial program, a sort-of joint venture between the rangers and the CIA."

"A training program?"

"Exactly." He gave me an approving nod. I'd said the right thing. After all, I was a spy, I was supposed to know about these things. "What we are-What we *were* doing was training special teams of expatriate North Vietnamese to go back into the North to stir things up. Blow bridges and dams. Stir up trouble."

"Right. Black ops. Of course." I nodded back at him like I knew all about it. Actually, I had heard a thing or too.

"Captain Harris was one of these gung-ho types. Probably too old to be out in the field, but that's what he wanted and he was good at it, so that's what he did."

"Trained groups of sappers."

"Yes. But he loved his little teams of black-pajama devils. They were his boys, his men. Problem was, though it was strictly against regulations, he went along with them."

"Into North Vietnam?!"

The Colonel held up a placating hand, "Well, not exactly. They always have to be-*had* to be-strictly ARVN missions. You know, international propaganda, world opinion, the whole mess. No U.S. involvement whatsoever. Harris knew all this, but he was so damn proud of his creations, you see. He wanted to go along in the flying boxcar, pat 'em on the ass and wave bye-bye as they jumped out into the dark over the Red River Delta or wherever."

"And *did* he go?"

"Damn straight. That's what all this is about." He swung a thumb towards the door behind which Ba Minh was waiting, probably with her ear cupped to the heavy wood.

"It was just before Christmas, 1961. The Da Nang airport. Night. Bad weather, lots of rain. Harris finaggles his way on board the plane that's supposed to wing eight of his finest northward over the DMZ and drop them with their black parachutes like little black poison seeds on enemy soil."

"Are they effective?" I asked, the words blurting out before I could stop myself.

He fixed me with a bleak look.

"Not to my knowledge."

"Do any of them ever come back?"

"Not that I know of. But I'm saying more than I should." He stood and began to pace in front of me.

"Anyway, none of that matters anyhow, because Harris and his merry band never get to North Vietnam. They never got anywhere. Boxcars aren't all that great in bad weather, and the damn thing slammed into an isolated hilltop north of Da Nang, killing everybody on board."

"God! Harris, too?"

The Colonel nodded wearily, taking off his wire-rimmed glasses and rubbing his eyes.

"Harris, too. Trouble is, the plane went down in an isolated area. Hard to get to, and the bad weather continues. We put some heat on to go in there and get the bodies, but it has to be ARVN personnel, and they're not too keen on going out into the bush, if you've noticed."

I gave him another knowing nod. This I did know; the Army of the Republic of South Vietnam was plagued with Buddhists who shot over the enemy's head out of principle, and Saigon Cowboys who hunkered down in their positions and never shot anybody at all.

"Not that there was much to find out there, anyway. The Flying Boxcar went smack into the rocky side of the hill, and there was nothing but bits and smears of bodies scattered everywhere. Very little that was big enough to be called a handful and nobody who could be recognized. We brought the bits down in bodybags and gave every coffin something, though they all were a little light. You throw in a brick or something and they don't open it up and nobody ever says anything. We buried the locals here, shipped something of Harris back and that was that."

"I don't get the problem."

"Well, like I said, Captain Harris had this wife. And Mrs. Harris couldn't understand how her husband died when all he'd ever told her was that he had a safe and cushy administrative desk job. The coffin shows up back in Kansas or wherever and somebody notices it's light and there's no way to truly identify the remains. We can't tell her the actual nature of his mission. We say something vague and unsatisfactory about a training flight, but that can't be true because he's in the army, not the air force. She's not sure he's even dead. In fact, she's more and more convincing herself that he's not. And we can't prove he is. So she demands all the coffins are opened."

Here the Colonel throws his hands up in the air. "Everybody else is cooperative, but your little princess out there sniffs blood."

"It's only natural. She has strong Buddhist feelings against-"

"Buddhist, my ass. She's a goddamn money-grubbing capitalist." The Colonel looked very upset, and his face started to shift to its former unhealthy flush. "See, her husband was the pilot on that flight. His remains are spread in all those boxes, just like the rest of them. Only difference is, she won't let us dig him up."

"What are you going to do?"

"It beats the hell out of me, Spec 5 Klawitter. I've got to open that coffin, but I don't know how to get it done. My hands are tied. I don't have the kind of money she's talking about. And if you start paying one, you have to pay them all."

"This is all about money?"

He handed back my Top Secret badge. "I'm going to have to pay her something. I just hope it's enough. Look, talk some sense into her. Tell her maybe a few thousand, that's it. You'll look like the hero, because right now, she's getting burial expenses and that's it."

By now he had his arm around my shoulder and was guiding me to the door. He nodded curtly to Ba Minh and moved us smartly out of the office. In another minute we were down the stairs and out on the busy street together. It was late morning and the air was already stale and hot.

She shrieked angrily for a *xe hoi taxi* and a little blue-and-cream Renault scuttled over to do her bidding. In an eye-blink we were rocketing back towards Cho Lon.

"I've got to get back to the base," I started hesitantly.

She reached for my arm, leaning close so that the nearest of her fantastic breasts brushed against me. "You not leave me. I need you help *now!*"

"Look, Co-or *Ba,* I should say-"

She burst into a loud crying jag, "I had to tell you he was my brother. All people say, if you knew I was married once, you not help me!"

"Never mind about that. Look, the Colonel said he will give you some money. He has to see that body."

"How much money?" Her eyes glittered bright and dark through her tears.

"Some thousands, even. Maybe two or three thousand."

"Three thousand, *my kim?*" *My kim* was Vietnamese for *American money.*

"Yes, *my kim.*"

Her face went dark and she spat in a scornful expression.

"It not enough!" she shouted. Her voice was so shrill the cabby in the front seat cringed like he'd been shot. She grabbed the front of my striped polo shirt and started shaking me as if that might improve my hearing.

"You know how much the widow of a downed Nationalist China airman get? $25,000 my kim! $25,000!"

I was struggling to catch up. "So this isn't really about the Buddhist problems with disturbing the dead?"

"I am a Buddhist," she shot back angrily, as if I was pond scum to suggest otherwise. "I also a business woman. American come over here, take advantage of Vietnam person. Take my husband, give me a few hundred my kim a month to live on. How I to live on a few hundred a month? How I to buy clothes and raise my daughter?!"

By now the cab had reached her address. The cabby sat hunched over his wheel, waiting for fate to determine where next he would ride.

"I don't know," I shouted back. We were in the kind of heated moment of truth where quiet conversation seemed less than adequate.

"You must help me."

"I've already helped you! They will give you $3,000 *my kim*!"

"*Khong phai*," she wailed. "No, no, no. You must help me more."

"What do you want me to do?!"

"Come up to apartment. We alone now. We be together. Then you write me letter to Mister President Johnson. He will give me my $25,000 *my kim*. Who knows? Maybe more, so not to be the fool!"

Before meeting Co Nhut, I guess I was your ordinary fool for love. I was the kind of guy who would stand on a doorstep for hours with a bouquet of wilted daisies, just to make a point about romance. I was a *guitar, jug of red wine, and thou* type of fellow, motivated to go to great lengths to get it off and get it on. The quest was as important as the conquest, and I didn't go much deeper than that in my relationship with women. But in that moment my lust for her flew out of the window, replaced by raw anger.

"You're nothing but a money-grubbing bitch!" I yelled in Vietnamese.

"Sao lam," the cabby agreed, leaning over the back of the front seat and nodding at me. *Very ugly, indeed!*

Ma Minh looked from one of us to the other, and for a moment I thought she would scratch us both to death with her long red fingernails. And then she opened the door and walked haughtily away.

I never saw her again. Nor did I find out if Mrs. Harris actually identified for certain whether any of the remains belonged to her husband. I was sure Harris wasn't her real name. Whether or not I was a Top Secret guy, Colonel Greene was no fool. I did my daily translations. Jack Black Flag moved on to make his slow way through the pages of L' Homme Revolté. The war continued its slow slide into inevitable chaos and ultimate loss.

It was actually almost thirty years later when I heard again about the exploits of the poor black-pajama troopers who'd been inspired to head back North and take up the uncertain life of terrorists. Some brief newspaper article, buried back on page two or three of the L.A. Times, caught my eye. No real news; officially, even that long after we'd been kicked out of Vietnam, the U.S. was still denying these guys existed or that such adventuring ever took place. That was the current problem; the few aging sods lucky enough to live through their terrorist days thought maybe the people who'd trained and flown them on their missions owed them some small pension, something more than *the thanks of a grateful nation.*

I thought about the beautiful and vicious Co Nhut with a dim reverberation of my old lust, and felt a twinge of nostalgia as I remembered once again Harvey's cynical wisdom. Back in 1965 I was already 25, a graduate student and a sort-of spy in the employ of the U.S. Army, yet I really knew nothing about the way things worked in life. Maybe I should have known better, but it was my first experience with that sort of thing, my waking realization of how different, like oil and water-and yet how inextricably tied-were the twin concepts of love and money.

What's it like to be stationed at a military intelligence outpost a few miles from the North Vietnamese border and a long way from home? Perhaps the following story will give you some idea.

THE DAY I WENT TO THE ORDERLY ROOM

By Wayne Robertson

It was in the early summer of 1964. I can't remember the exact date, but I'm pretty sure it was some time in April or May. I arrived in Vietnam in March of '64, and after a few days of orientation at Davis Station in Saigon, I was sent up to Phu Bai.

I hadn't been at Phu Bai long and was still trying to get settled in. One of the NCO's who gave the FNG (Fucking New Guy) orientation said that there were about 20,000 to 25,000 American troops in Vietnam at that time. Most of them were in an advisory role to the South Vietnamese Military. Of course, our unit was doing some 'research' on radio waves.

Phu Bai was the most laid-back post I had been on in my long and illustrious two-year army career. It seemed like I almost never saw an officer, and the NCO's mostly acted like real people, instead of the military tyrants I had seen in boot camp and other posts. At the end of the month, there were always some field grade officers that would find a reason to come and inspect our outpost. The scuttlebutt among the troops was that they had to visit the field locations long enough to qualify for their combat pay. None of us enlisted pukes who worked there ever could grasp how the officers could qualify for combat pay for being on the ground in Phu Bai for 15 minutes a month. Back then, enlisted ranks didn't get combat pay; it was still a year away. But you could always tell when one of the VIP's was on the post, because there would be two Huey gun ships circling overhead. Those damn choppers would play hell with some of the radio frequencies, so when I saw the Huey's, I always managed to find somewhere else that I needed to be.

In general, I liked the laid-back atmosphere of Phu Bai, because the strict structure that was required of most military environments had not appealed to me very much. I just wanted to do my job, finish my tour, and go home with as little fuss as possible. With that in mind, you might wonder what catastrophic event might cause me to actually make a trip to the orderly room on my own.

I was put on the day trick when I arrived at Phu Bai. This was a major change for me. For some reason, every time in the past when someone was needed to work the dark shifts, it always seemed to end up being me. I never could figure out why everyone thought I looked like a night person. Later on, when I was moved back down to Davis Station, I was put on the swing trick. But while at Phu Bai, I finally got to work days. I even had an early sked to make, which got me out of the morning formation early. I was able to avoid listening to a bunch of boring announcements and didn't have to police the area. I would go in to OPS to make my sked and then go to breakfast about the time the rest of the formation finished up. Life was good, at least as good as it was going to get, living that close to the DMZ. (ed note: Phu Bai was only a few kilometers south of the demilitarized zone separating North from South Vietnam.)

One Wednesday, I had the day off. I'd helped close the EM club down the night before. Some jarhead Marine PFC had decided he was going to get the big Texan (that's me) drunk. Well, I'm here to tell you that seagoing bellhop accomplished his mission, even though I still managed, somehow to get to my bunk. After sleeping late the next morning, I woke with a pounding in my head and a taste in my mouth that reminded me of a mud bog in which I had seen two water buffalo wallowing the day before. I would have bet money that the water they were giving me to chase down the scotch last night came from downstream of that buffalo wallow. As the glaze slowly started to clear from my mind, I realized that I had not eaten since yesterday at lunch, and that seemed to compound the problem. I did have one first-class, ass-kicking hangover. Man, I sure hoped that jarhead was feeling as bad as I was.

I went through the 3 S's (shit, showered & shaved) and, with about half a tube of toothpaste, managed to get most of that buffalo wallow out of my mouth. A cap, T-shirt, fatigue pants, and boots were always the uniform of the day, and I somehow managed to make myself presentable. By now, I was starting to feel almost human, though I was hungry enough to challenge a she-wolf for that last morsel of carrion. I left the barracks and headed for the mess hall where I hoped to find a cup of coffee and possibly some leftovers. Sometimes, when the mess sergeant was in a good mood, he would even let us raid the refrigerator.

Now how many times have you ever seen a mess sergeant in that good a mood? Most of the time, our mess sergeant was an alright guy, but sometimes he was…well, a mess sergeant. I just took it as a matter of course that part of his job was being pissed off at PFC grade enlisted pukes like me.

Well, when I got there, the old mess sergeant was in rare form. He was yelling stomping his feet, waving his arms and cussing a blue streak. You would have through somebody had jumped up and taken a dump on his brand-new stainless steel company-sized grill. I never did find out what was bothering him, and probably didn't want to know, but something had definitely pissed him off. The Vietnamese civilians that we hired to do KP duty for us were running and scampering about, cleaning and shining everything as they went.

So my timing certainly wasn't the best as I walked in the door and said, "Hi Sarge," in the best, most-cheerful late morning, hung-over, hungry-as-a-bear voice that I could muster under the circumstances.

"Now, just who the hell do you think you are?!", he bellowed. "You some kind of prima donna that thinks he can walk in here after chow time and be served at his leisure?"

"No, Sarge, I just wanted a cup of your delicious burnt coffee," I replied, realizing there was no way in hell I was going to get anything out of him. He promptly threw my ass out of the mess hall. He followed me a short distance, spewing a long list of colorful expletives as only a mess sergeant can. I probably shouldn't have said his coffee was burnt, but I always did have a penchant for mouthing off when silence would have served me better.

I toyed briefly with the idea of going into operations where they always had a pot of coffee on. But I quickly abandoned that idea, deciding they would probably just put me to work, even though it was my day off. Listening to a squawking radio didn't sound much like headache therapy to me, so I moseyed on back toward the EM club, hoping they might be getting ready for the day's business by now and have a pot of coffee on.

As I was crossing the compound, heading away from the mess hall, a sudden commotion caught my attention, and I turned to check it out. It was break time for the Vietnamese civilians working in the mess hall, and a bunch of them were headed for the latrine. They ware talking loudly, waving their arms and gesturing in a comical manner that UI took to be their impression of the mess sergeant. Amused, I turned back towards my quest for a cup of coffee to soothe my pounding head. At that moment, something caught my eye in the distance. It was back over the top of the mess hall. A small speck in the sky was moving rapidly towards the compound. It had to be an aircraft of some type, but the only aircraft I ever saw around Phu Bai were the Hueys and an occasional C-123 (flying boxcar). This plane was hugging the ground and moving in our direction. It was coming fast, very fast, and getting closer. Damn, I thought, maybe it was an F105 or one of those new F4 Phantoms the U.S. Navy had. It definitely had my attention. It was closer now. It turned its nose down slightly and came straight at us. My mind was racing. The angle of its descent toward the compound suggested a bombing or strafing run. What the hell could it be? The South Vietnamese didn't have any jets, so it couldn't be them. Hell, everybody knew the North Vietnamese didn't have much of an air force, so it couldn't be them.

Maybe, I thought, a young U.S. Air Force pilot was practicing. *Practicing, my ass!,* I thought, *If that thing keeps coming, I'm headed for cover!* I looked quickly around to see where the closest cover might be, and to check out what everybody else was doing. There wasn't anybody else. The compound was deserted. There wasn't another soul in sight, not even the ever-present Vietnamese construction workers.

Well, that ripped it; I was in a full-blown panic. I looked up towards the plane, and had actually started to turn to run when it suddenly pulled up and banked sharply to the left. It made a 180 degree turn and hauled ass back the way it had came, toward Laos. For an instant, after it had pulled up and was turning, the plane presented its bottom side in a perfect dark silhouette against a clear blue sky. It had the swept-back wings and tail of a jet fighter. Its profile was similar to but not quite exactly that of the F-86 Sabre jet that I had seen in Korean War movies. *Wait a minute now,* I thought to myself, *the U.S. hadn't used F-86's in over a decade. It couldn't be ours!* My heart was really pounding now. It dawned on me that it looked like a MIG-15 or maybe a MIG-17. *Could it be?* I had seen plenty of them in the old Korean War movies as well. *Could some North Vietnamese pilot have gone temporarily insane or gotten lost or something?* The rush was subsiding as I watched what was now a speck in the sky disappear in the distance as it moved West North West back towards the mountains of Laos. *Screw the coffee,* I thought, *I need a drink!*

I found my way back to the EM club, which, much to my relief, was now open. I sat down at the bar.

"What can I get you this morning?" the bartender asked.

"Drunk," I replied flatly.

"Sorry, can't serve alcohol this early. Coffee or soda is the best I can do," he said with a smile.

"Coffee, then," I replied. "Make it strong and black. And don't be so damn cheerful."

He poured the coffee with another smile and left me sitting at the bar with both hands wrapped securely around the coffee cup, as if trying to protect it from anyone who might try to take it away from me. I sipped on the black nectar and reran the details of those few seconds when I had watched the plane through my head. *Let's think this thing through now,* I thought. During my duty at Ft. Carson, I'd been so bored that I'd entertained the thought of applying for flight school. I'd passed the flight physical with near-perfect vision. My head was clear—hurting, but clear. The weather was clear, too, with unlimited visibility. *Damn it, I knew what I saw! I had not imagined it!*

At about that time, some of the guys stuck their heads in the door, looking for the jarhead who had gotten me so wasted the night before. I said I hadn't seen him since the night before. "Hope his head is hurting as bad as mine," I groaned. They laughed and went on their way. But just about the time they left, I noticed some movement and a slight groan from underneath a table in the back corner. For a moment, I thought it was the jarhead, and that I might have left him worse off than I was, but I was disappointed. It was a buck sergeant who worked in the motor pool. He'd gotten so drunk the night before that his buddies pushed him into a corner to let him sleep it off. I helped him up to the bar and bought him a cup of coffee. Now there were two of us sitting at the bar, both with our hands wrapped securely around our coffee cups and our heads bowed somewhat, as if in prayer.

After a few minutes of silently nursing our coffee, he squinted over at me with a pained expression. "What day is this?" he asked.

"Wednesday," I replied with a similar expression on my own face.

"Damn. I'll get chewed out for this…maybe even busted…"

"I just had an interesting experience," I said. In my current state, I thought it might clear things up to discuss what had just happened. He just looked at me with an even more pained expression that told me it wasn't a good idea. I decided not to pursue it. After a long silence and a second cup of coffee, he started showing signs of life and becoming more amiable. We developed an excuse for him that might save him from a demotion. I agreed that I would be his witness; he was just too sick to function. In return, he had to listen to my story.

If I thought he wouldn't be impressed by my tale of the swooping airplane, I was wrong.

"Holy Shit!" he cried, "you better go tell somebody in the orderly room!"

The orderly room. Those words took me back a bit. Officers and NCOs hung out in the orderly room. The idea of voluntarily going over there didn't fit in with my policy of doing my job with as little fuss as possible. The more I thought about it, the more preposterous the whole story sounded. I suggested that the guys in the orderly room would get a really good laugh out of this one. Here we sat, two guys nursing serious hangovers and trying to make earth-shaking decisions of enormous magnitude. But it didn't solve my problem; *should I go over to the orderly room with my story of the interloping MIG, or not?* We sat and tried to think it through.

"Man," the buck sergeant finally said, "If that really was a MIG, and you didn't report it, and it went off and shot some poor G.I. or something…" I knew I was screwed. In one sentence he had put both the patriotic as well as the do-your-duty trips on me.

I finished my coffee and reluctantly headed toward the orderly room. As I entered, one of the clerks looked up and asked me what I wanted.

"Well," I said, "I've just seen something I think maybe I should report…"

"Yeah? What's that?"

"A MIG," I replied.

The clerk gave me an expression that said he'd thought he'd heard all the bullshit stories, but this was a new wrinkle. "Hey, Sarge," he said. "You need to handle this one."

Well, here we go, I thought. I told my story, but as I went through the details I could see the clerk and the sergeant were giving each other knowing looks, the kind with the slight curl coming to their lips. The sergeant would ask me a question from time to time. I almost expected him to ask if the plane was piloted by a pink elephant.

Part way through the story, an officer came over to see what the stir was about. He listened quietly, and, after I was through, he told the clerk to type it up and send it to headquarters.

"Thank you, son," he said. "If they have any questions, we'll call you back to the orderly room."

I was never called back in, and I never heard any more about it. I'm sure it got catalogued and filed in the round file cabinet with the open mouth. I couldn't tell if the officer thought I was just some smart-ass trying to stir something up, or if he thought I simply didn't know what I was talking about. But I did get the very strong impression that he wanted that story to die quickly.

After that, whenever I was walking across the compound, my eyes would always be pulled in the direction of Laos. I often wondered about that MIG, where it had come from and where it was going. I found out later that the jarhead had gone on sick call that morning, and that brought a smile to my face. It is all rolled up together in my memory...the angry mess hall sergeant, the hung-over motor pool sergeant, the jarhead who tried to drink me under the table, and the MIG from out of nowhere. I never saw another MIG, though. Thank God for that. I sure would have hated to go back to the orderly room.

Here's another story from Torii station on Okinawa. Stay in the army long enough and you might be surprised at some of the people you meet.

A MARINE GETS FISHED

By Hal Castle

Y'all got quirks? Most folks do. Some kind of little thing they do that may seem out of place to others. One of mine is popping my knuckles at the wrong time. Another is constantly bouncing my legs while sitting. This is a true story of two people, the juxtaposition of whose quirks helped me fish—that is, *hustle*—one of the greatest hustlers the country has ever seen.

It was sometime in 1968. I was back in Okinawa from one of my trips to Southeastern Asia. I had some time on my hands before I had to go back on shift. One afternoon, I went down to the Brown Derby bar, which was just off Kadena Circle. As I came in, I noticed two young Marines, in uniform, at the bar.

One of the Marines said something to me in Tex-Mex. That was understandable; I had a deep tan, dark wavy hair and a big moustache. But I didn't know any Tex-Mex, so I just said, "Huh?" I explained I didn't know much more than *cerveza* and *mas cerveza*. The one spoke pretty fair English, and we hit it off well. I asked what they were doing in a bar while on duty, and they replied they had just gotten off work and were having a brew before going up-island. They worked at the boat basin down by the army airfield, checking out boats to anyone who wanted one and had a license to operate the boat. They also gave the Small Boat Certification Test. A lot of what they did was give instructions on small boat operation to Marines who were on the island for R&R, or who were getting ready to go to Vietnam and had a day or two off and wanted to go fishing.

My new friend told me he also taught Marines how to play golf. He had been a caddy at a big golf club in Texas when he got drafted. He supplemented his income by hustling the rich gringos who played at the club. He tried to keep it up while on active duty, because he was sending money home. He figured, as he'd been drafted into the Marines, for once the Marines had picked the right guy for the job. He was using his talents to help other Marines learn something besides breaking things and killing people.

He would go up-island and teach Marines the basics of golf. Then they would come down to the Kadena or Machinato courses and play. When he wasn't teaching, he would play with other Americans or Japanese.

"So if you want to play" he offered, "just come down to the basin and let me know. We can go for ten cents a stroke, fifty cents a hole, or 5 bucks for the game. And I'll just play using only one or two clubs."

We were getting on okay when he said, "I bet my buddy here can blow smoke out of his ear. I'll bet you a round of beers on it."

I knew I was being hustled, but I agreed anyway. "Yeah, I think you're blowing it out your ass. You're on!"

So his buddy, the other Marine, lit up a great big stogie and got it going real good. Then he took a hit that would make most Mary Jane tokers gaga at the sheer volume his lungs could hold. He clamped one big Iowa plowboy hand over his nose and mouth and turned red in the face. And then a stream of cigar smoke came out of his right ear. Honest, it came directly out of his ear.

I ordered a round of Orion for the three of us, and he told me the story. The poor guy had been in Vietnam when something blew up close to him, rupturing everything inside from his Eustachian tube to his throat. The Marines had reassigned him to Special Services while they tried to figure out what to do with him. He was helping his pal, the golf hustler. He carried the golf clubs and kept the small boat hulls clear of sea shells. He fixed the ropes when they snapped or became tangled.

"He's a good guy, for a gringo," the hustler said with a friendly smile. "I hope they let him stay on with me."

One of the hostesses in the bar had a quirk of her own. She would rub her shapely thigh, saying "Hai, Hai!" to everything anyone said to her. We called her Itchy Knee San. She said she was a village girl, just working to make a little money for the family, and she was going to go home at the earliest opportunity. At least, that's what she said.

I thought she was far too good-looking and too young for the likes of the Brown Derby's normal clientele. Mama San or the Okinawa Mafia were probably grooming her for work at one of the swanky Senior Officer hangouts or one of the clubs frequented by the rich Japanese. Itchy Knee San never went upstairs with a man, and all she ever had to drink was the Sontori brand White Horse scotch-laced tea drink, at about a dollar a pop.

As our time in the bar progressed, she and the young Marine started to hit it off. Soon he was buying an occasional scotch for her. I knew it was just tea with a hint of scotch flavor, but I didn't say anything. He would say something to Itchy and she would giggle, rub her thigh and say, "Hai, Hai, Maline Ree!" The Derby was pretty tame at mid-afternoon during the week, and I was getting bored. We had a few more laughs and I decided to mosey on to another bar.

A day or two later I met my hustler acquaintance over at the Machinato Golf Course. Our Trick was on break, and I was taking a walk with my friend and mentor, Sergeant First Class Tom Beaven. I wasn't much of a golfer, and neither was Tom, but in his mind he was right up there with Ben Hogan. And Tom had another problem…he loved to bet on anything. When I introduced him to the hustler, he felt he'd found a sure mark; after all, what Tex-Mex out of San Antonio could possibly know how to play golf like an Army Security Agency Sergeant First Class? When the hustler suggested the dime/half-dollar/five dollars challenge to him, Tom bit like a great white shark on a flopping chicken. He bit hard and set the hook himself.

The Machinato course on Okinawa has a difficult 1st hole, and only gets more difficult from there on. The first tee shot has to go between two hills. Then there is a dog-leg to the right. Many golfers look at it on the map and try to shoot over the right hill. They either don't make it, or they wind up in the rough on the back side. Tom teed off right between the hills, a good first shot. The Tex-Mex hustler used a long iron shot to go right over the hill. Tom was so sure of his victory that he asked for his shot and hole money right there. He was convinced the hustler's ball was in a really bad lie. Instead, the hustler suggested they double the bet. Tom went for that, hook, line and sinker.

When we got to Tom's ball, we saw he had a good lie for an approach. He might make par, or even a birdie. As for the hustler's ball, well, it was right in the center of the fairway. He chipped on the green and made his putt for a birdie. Tom was so upset that he blew his approach and his putt and had to settle for a bogie. So the 70 cent hole cost him a buck-twenty.

It continued in the same way. The hustler kept egging Tom on, and he bit on dumber and dumber bets. On the 8th hole, when Tom finally wouldn't bite on a particularly foolish bet, the hustler suggested that the loser of this hole would buy a round at the 19th for each stroke he would lose. The hustler lost the hole and two strokes, so he owed three beers. But by the end of the game, he could have gotten the entire bar drunk with the money he took off of Tom Beaven.

As we were continuing the round, the hustler started asking me how he could get Itchy into the sack. "Every time I get close, she goes into her thigh-rubbing *Hai Hai* thing," he complained.

"Just talk to her about it," I replied.

"I don't speak Japanese, and she don't speak English or Tex-Mex."

"I don't see what I could do…"

"Maybe you could talk to Mama San about it? I would make it worth your while, buy you a couple of beers, maybe more…"

I thought it over. I never liked to lose a bet, and was still thinking about the Marine blowing smoke out of his ear, "I'll see what I can come up with," I said. "Meet me at the Derby tomorrow at 1700 hours, after I get off shift and before the place gets too crowded with Zoomie types."

He showed up the next day, salivating over the idea of Itchy in the sack, so eager it looked like his tongue was dragging on the floor.

"Here's what you do," I instructed. "You tell her *Tak San Chisai Tamadatchi.*"

He bought a few rounds of beer while I instructed him until he had the pronunciation down pat. I grabbed my right arm on the biceps with my left hand. I curled the forearm up and made a fist. "You know," I said, "Like a burro, a lot of little friend... *Tak San Chisai Tamadatchi!*"

He ordered a double scotch for me, but I stopped Mama San from pouring it. "Keep it for later," I told her with a wink. "It's going to taste much better."

Itchy Knee San hadn't yet made an appearance, so the hustler came over and ordered us another round of beers and scotch. I was still nursing my last beer, so I told Mama San to hold my drinks for later. The hustler wrapped himself around his double White Horse, made a horrible face, grabbed his Orion and started chugging.

"Hey, slow down," I advised. "You're going to be too drunk to remember the words. And, even if you do, you won't be able to get it up for Itchy." But my advice didn't do any good. He ordered each of us another round and went back to his own table, lost in his schemes of wooing and winning the body if not the soul of Itchy Knee San.

The lady herself showed up about 1830, and by then the hustler was in sorry shape. She spied him and went directly to his table. She gave him a lingering peck on the cheek and then went around the table to greet the rest of her regular friends. After giving us our greetings, she returned to the hustler, who was in sorry shape, barely able to sit up. She sat next to him and they leaned close together and did the things young would-be lovers do in public places. A waitress came over with

Itchy's drink and the hustler put a large lump of money on the tray to cover all the drinks he'd ordered.

I took a stogie from my pocket and lit it. I felt ready for revenge.

But now the hustler was ready to make his own move. "*Tak San Chisi Tamadachi!*" he cried. "I've got *Tak San Chisi Tamadachi!*"

At this, Itchy jumped up and screamed at the top of her lungs. She grabbed her purse and raced out the door. The hustler had told her—and everyone else in the bar—that he was infested with a case of the crabs. But he didn't know this. He leapt to his feet and rushed over to Mama San, yelling, "What happened? Where is she?"

Maybe it's just my perverted sense of humor, but here's where I thought it got really funny. In the Japanese counting system, Itchy is One, Knee is Two, and San is Three. When Mama San replied, she said, "*Itchi Knee San She Go!*" Of course, she was saying that Itchy had left. But, phonetically in Japanese, She means Four, and Go means Five. One-Two-Three-Four-Five! That was so hilarious to me that I couldn't stop laughing.

That evening, the crowd at the Brown Derby couldn't talk about anything but the hostess who ran out of the bar after her suitor told her he had a massive case of the crabs. There it was. I got hustled by, and then managed to hustle, a young Marine who would go on to become a legend among professional golfers. That night he surely was one "Mad Mexican", the then Marine Lance Corporal, Lee Trevino.

After a tour in Vietnam, an assignment at one of the ASA listening posts in Thailand could seem like a blessed relief, even if you were still doing the same work. Thailand was just as remote and exotic, the culture as old and rich in traditions, the people arguably as finely shaped and attractive.

COMPLICATED SEX

By Ken Jones

In 1973, I was stationed about as close to paradise as you can get in this man's army and that is Chaing Mai, Thailand. Back then, the headquarters of the 7th RRFS was just south of the city of Udon Thani, also called Udorn, a city of about 70,000 in the northcentral part of the country and about 30 kilometers from the Mekong River which at that point separates Thailand from Laos. There were three Radio Direction Finding sites, one at the Field Station, one in Ubon, which was to the southeast of Udorn and nearer to where Laos, Cambodia and Thailand meet…and one in the paradise that was Chaing Mai.

Chaing Mai was a showplace Det for all of Southeast Asia. Chaing Mai is in the mountains; the city is beautiful and the climate is pleasant. And the girls…well, the girls are drop-dead gorgeous.

Naturally, I found the duty there was great. I was one of two NCOs. We had a radio Mech, a Crypto Mech, a Teletype Mech, a designated house "mom", and two operators (E-4 and E-5) for four tricks. We had a ten-bedroom house, a bar, a living room, a maid, a cook and a bartender. We drew allowances of about $300 per month for rations and living expenses, and the house bill usually ran $80-90 a month.

We were in Thailand to support the U.S. effort in Vietnam. The majority of the military were Air Force, but the Army had various Signal,

Supply, Engineering, and Special forces—and, of course, ASA units—stationed around the country. The largest bases were in Satahip, a supply depot on the southern coast, and Korat, a large Signal Corps and Combat Engineer Base in south central Thailand. Like Vietnam, the normal army tour in Thailand was 12 months. But some found the life there so heavenly that they extended their tours in 6-month increments. There were guys who had stayed there as long as 5 years. For us guys in the ASA, the duty was easy, the mission was fun and exciting, and it beat painting rocks at Fort Hood, Texas. Of course, if a trooper found a good-looking lady to warm his bed, that didn't harm the picture, either.

When you take a young and lusty bunch of soldiers and put them in such an environment, the unexpected not only can happen, but it is likely. Here's an unlikely story I heard when I was stationed at Chaing Mai.

Now our little corner of Thailand was popular as a place to buy souvenirs, and sometimes guys would come in from other Dets just to take a break and have a little taste of heaven. First Sergeant Stanton had come up to Chaing Mai from his station at Udorn, which is near where Laos, Cambodia and Thailand meet.

Since he felt he needed to conduct some business (other than souvenir shopping) while he was with us, he decided to give Bill Herr, the senior Spec 5's and myself some leadership training. This training mostly consisted of us gathering at the house bar for several rounds of Singha beers. And, since nominally the subject was leadership, he said he'd tell us a story to illustrate how a Non Commissioned Officer must be able to think on his feet.

It started, he said, one day at the field station when an 05H came in to his office to apply to marry his sweet thing. Now the army in general, and even a security-minded outfit like the ASA, tends to look the other way when the troopers engage in casual romance with the local beauties. However, when a young man gets serious enough to announce he wishes to formalize a personal relationship of this sort, it becomes entirely something else.

Requests like this can be complicated, for human emotion is involved on one side, and army intelligence security clearances on the other. NCO's and Company Commanders take their responsibilities seriously, and in some respects consider themselves surrogate father figures. In this respect, their troopers are their children, and a request to marry is serious business. Then too, marrying a local was the surest way to lose a security clearance. Nobody likes to lose an experienced 05H, so Stanton got down to the business of interviewing the operator with some reluctance.

"Mmmm," he said, reviewing the young man's file on the desk in front of him. "Says here you re-upped about 6 months ago."

"That's right, sir."

His voice took on a sterner tone, "And what did you do with all that money you got to reenlist?"

The 05H's face flushed, "Well…you know, we needed a TV set…"

"For the hooch?"

"Uhh—yes, sir…and there were other necessities."

"Furniture, clothes, hairspray from the PX?"

The 05H nodded, looking down at his hands.

Stanton decided not to follow that line of reasoning any further. He felt some sympathy for the young man. The people of Thailand are lean and graceful, and their culture is a very old and sophisticated one. Stanton knew, once you got past the cultural differences, the women of Thailand could be beautiful, excellent and willing lovers, and inexpensive by American standards. He also knew that, once they had a guy on the hook, they reeled him in hard.

"How long have you been living with your *tee loc?*"

The young man flushed an even brighter red, knowing the Thai word for 'true love'. "Uhh…about 10 months, sir."

"Okay. You know, with your clearance, this never, never, never should happen."

"Sir, I have the right—"

Stanton waved the young man silent before he could say anything they both might regret.

"I know. You have the right. But it is also company policy that the Commander interviews the object of your affections. Will you bring her in if I set it up?"

"Yes, sir!" The young man beamed, saluted and rushed out of the room.

Two weeks later, Stanton said, the 05H showed up with his beaming fiancée in tow for their interview with the Commander. By this time, we all were wondering where the story was going. Guys, even guys with Top Secret clearances, were known to fall for the local beauties and to marry them. There didn't seem much of a story in that.

I ordered another round of Singha's, "And so they lived together forever in bliss and happiness in their suburban hooch outside of Bangkok?"

"Not exactly," Stanton grinned. "See, this is where the NCO's leadership in action roll comes into play. I tell you, that Thai girl looked mighty familiar to me. I let the couple go in for their interview, but meanwhile I was racking my brain in a mighty and intense way. I knew I'd seen her before—and then it came to me! I'd read an article in the Bangkok Post, all about the first sex change to be performed in Thailand."

"Naw," I said. "It wasn't *her?!* That didn't really happen?!"

Stanton raised his beer bottle in our direction, a happy salute. "There was her picture in the paper and everything. It was the same person!"

Stanton had to rustle around a bit, but he found the article and showed it to the Commander. By the time he found it, the interview was over, but the ceremony hadn't yet been performed. There was another brief but intense meeting in the Commander's office, and then they made sure the stunned and mortally embarrassed young trooper was shipped off to Korat or somewhere...somewhere far, far away. He was hooked hard, all right, and not as innocent as he made out to be. Later they found out he'd used his re-up bonus for the operation.

In the 1960s, military intelligence mirrored the general sociological atti-
tudes in America with regard to gays and lesbians. The army had special inter-
nal investigating units that strove to ferret out deviant sexual behavior. The
rumor was, they went so far as to set up entrapping situations in bars and
nightclubs. Be that as it may, in those times to be called a gay man was an
insult to one who was straight. And, as ever, there was a wealth of jokes and
humorous stories built up around sexual situations.

SITTING ON THE CURB IN TORII

By Tom Kemper

If you are U.S. Army, you probably know the manhood of anyone who joins the Air Force has historically been suspect. This idea may have surfaced because Air Force people are thought to not bear the brunt of war, but rather to flit about on the edges of the battlefield, if they even get that close. It is true that caring for an aircraft has a mechanical ring to it, while caring for a rifle implies survival, ruggedness and manly ways. But it is perhaps going overboard to constantly refer to the Wild Blue Yonder Gang as flyboys or zoomies.

The scene is Torii Station. After sojourns at Phu Bai, South Vietnam, and An-Jang-Ri, Korea, I was assigned to the 51st United States Army Security Agency Special Operations Command in Sobe, Okinawa. It was a joint services operation, more or less owned by NSA. Everyone but the Coast Guard was there, but who knows? Maybe they were, too. A Torii is a gate to a Japanese Temple, and we had one. (A gate, not a temple) Sobe was a small village on the west side of the narrow island. It was a craggy sort of island, formed by volcanic action that took place eons before we got there. The interior had sugar cane and pineapple fields, but the rest of the economy was military. The blue-green and aqua waters of the China Sea, and the angry deep blue waters of the Pacific bracketed us.

Before I continue this sad tale of inter-service insensitivity (in the olden days, before PC, we would have called it a friendly rivalry), I must digress to a Chinese linguist I met only briefly at Torii, just before he was transferred to Taiwan. I do not remember this lingie's name, but he was from South Carolina and had colorful opinions about everything. What there is about him that sticks in my memory was his version of the war (and of international relations in general). His basic idea was that we should bomb North Vietnam flat and pave it. "Shoot," he would say, "we got a pavin' company in Columbia, Sath Cahlina could do the job in about a month. Think of the runway we would have, pointin' right at China!"

Beyond his somewhat simplistic solution to international problems, this Chinese lingie had strong opinions about almost everything in society, from zoomies to gays. In fact, he'd combined both these subjects in a memorable character he'd invented and named Captain Lance Sterling, faggot F-105 Thunderchief pilot. He'd create numerous scenarios for the gay Captain and drew a fierce sort of joy from the imagined embarrassment Lance brought to the officials of the U.S. Air Force. He thought up a scenario in which an Air Force Public Relations specialist escorts a reporter down the flight line at Danang. As they passed the various F-105's, the PR guy intoned, "This is Captain Barnes' plane, *The Avenger*. And here is Major Lebowski's plane, *The Tiger*. Captain Smith's plane, *The Hammer*."

At this point the reporter interrupts, "Uhh…who flies the pink one?"

"Oh, that's Captain Sterling's plane, *The Tinkerbell*." The PR guy hurries the reporter along without further comment. The adventures of Lance Sterling, always good for a howl. On another occasion, when returning from North Vietnam, Sterling's group commander told them all to dump any unused ordnance, as it is unhealthy to land with bombs under the wings. Most diverted out to sea, but Sterling said he had a target of opportunity.

"Tinkerbell, where are you going!"

"Starting bombing run."

"Tinkerbell, for God's sake, that's a hospital!"

"Oh, Jesus, I love this."

It was some months later, and my Defense Language Institute roommate and I were passing time in the stag bar at Torii. This bar featured a big-time bowling machine. It wasn't one of those computer joystick games, but one where you had to roll a ball down a wooden lane to knock down suspended pins. We were bowling two Air Force NCO's for drinks, and we all were pretty much into it. I remember I was drinking Jack on the rocks and my friend was going along with Johnny Walker. We were ahead, with drinks stacked up on the bar, when I decided to crank the zoomies a bit.

"Did you ever hear of Lance Sterling...?" I started.

"No, never did" one of the flyboys replied.

"Faggot Thunderchief pilot," I said casually. "Flies the Tinkerbell."

Now, at the time, there were some NATO codewords describing Russian aircraft, and one of the MiGs, probably the 19 or the 21 was designated "Faggot". These have long been declassified, but not then.

The outraged replies were a pleasure to the ear. All the shouting and pointing! You would have thought I'd just handed over nuclear technology to the Sultan of Brunei.

"Come on, fellows" I replied, "you Air Force guys yourselves call the old Russian MiG's 'Faggots.' This is different."

Now I was on a roll. "Not only that" I said, "but in Old English, a faggot is a bundle of sticks. And, of course, in current slang, a faggot is a homosexual."

This last comment really unnerved them. You'd have thought I'd betrayed the Intergalactic League by siding with the Death Star. It certainly didn't do anything good for the zoomies bowling skills. By the time we decided to move on, my friend and I still had about 15 untouched drinks on the bar.

We left the bar, full of good booze and high spirits. We were both going back to the barracks, but we veered like a two-fish school toward the front gate. We had apparently both decided independently to go to town. At that point we sat down on the curb by the front gate, and each tried to convince the other that that he was too drunk to go to town. Well, alcohol-fueled logic never does work, so we got up and continued on our mission.

He headed over to a restaurant in Kadena Circle to wait for his girl-friend to get off work. He told me the next day that he'd had some ice tea and egg foo yung and threw up. For myself, I remember sitting down in a skoshi cab and saying, "Futenma." They had a great down-scale massage parlor down there, but I'd had so much to drink, I'm not sure I ever got there. If I did, I certainly don't remember any of the details. For all I know, the cab driver could have dumped me in a ditch outside the gate. Anyway, I did wake up the next morning in my bunk at Company C. And, for all I know, Captain Lance Sterling still flits through the skies in his pink Thunderchief, ever ready to entertain his friends and provide discomfort to the enemies of the democratic free world.

Manhood being such an important part of the man, here's a painful memory from an ASA listening post in the hills of Central Vietnam.

GETTING SHAFTED

By Hal Castle

The tales that could be told about some of the Army Security Agency (ASA) folks that I knew "in the Nam" would not be appropriate for *Today's Army*, but here goes one.

A guy named Doug Seals (noooo relation to the noted protestor of the time), and a couple of 'listees (enlisted men) who shall remain unnamed were all in one of those hilltop hangouts the ASA Special Operations Detachments (ASA SOD) used to man, along with regular Special Forces teams. There were the oddly bunkered CONEX containers, with a shelf or two welded inside on one wall to hold the intercept radios and the Hallicrafters KWM-7 HF transceivers. On the other wall was sometimes welded a steel bed frame.

The site was selected for its 360-degree visibility of the valleys below, where the Montagnard villagers lived and worked their fields and paddies, moving at the pace of the water buffaloes they followed. The view in good weather was nothing less than spectacular–the verdant hardwood forests, the green of the growing rice, tea and coffee plants, the banana trees–all symbols of and essential to a way of life that was centuries old. It's location offered good radio reception (what we called 'hear-ability'), some security...but, unfortunately, its exposure made it a good target.

Now old Doug was rumored to be the Best-Hung White Boy in Special Forces. And he loved to sleep buck naked to impress the "yard" women and girls who came by to cook, clean, hang out and whatever. This wasn't seen as too strange, since you had to adapt to the climate. Though it was "Dry Season", the weather was still hot and humid up there in the Central Highlands. Where were we going to find underwear, anyway, that wouldn't rot in a week?

One young Hawg, known to many of us, used to sleep in jungle boots and cut-off jungle fatigue pants. The theory was that one could run faster semi-bare-assed than totally barefooted. One day, after a grueling 14 hours of radio intercept work, this young Hawg was catching a few zees in one of the CONEX shelters. Doug Seal was dozing in the other bunker while the third ASA guy was "knobbing" for any signal traffic he could find on the intercept radio, and an A Team was spread around.

The site started taking probing rounds, and then a couple of 122 mm rounds came in with the *Whooooo whizzzzz ker-CRUMP!* kind of noise that they make. All able-bodied men headed for their assigned defensive positions, including buck-naked Doug Seals who was sporting a magnificent urinary boner. Seal took a header into the M-60 pit and…do you all remember the old concertina wire we had? Not the razor wire variety, the stuff with the really long and nasty spikes that looked like a spur on a fighting rooster. Remember that stuff?

Well, Doug, during his header into the M-60 pit, didn't quite get the elevation and angle he really needed on launch, and one of those big old nasty spikes reached out and speared his *Best Hung White Boy In SF* member. He wailed with real fear in his voice, "Help me, please!!" No one rightly knew if it was fear of being shot or fear for his crank, but that wasn't the time to find out.

The place was under fire, and we didn't really have time to save someone's dick while we were worried about saving all our asses, so, despite all Doug's screams and pleas, we went about the business of securing our own positions, looking for targets, and so on.

After a while, it seemed it was more an incident of harassment than an all-out attack. There were a few remotely launched 122's and bamboo mortars, along with one or two rifles being fired just to let us know that

Charles was temporarily in the AO. After a while, *just possibly* extended by the leadership beyond normal SOP, the heightened state of alert was lowered to the point where we could attend the *BHWBISF.*

The team medic, playing to an audience of all the Americans and many of the 'yards, snipped the spike off the main wire strand with a great deal of care, all the while apologizing with an assortment of sniggers, chortles and guffaws, "Scuze me, Sergeant Seals, this is gonna hurt just a little bit, but I gotta give you a tetanus shot at the point of injury, 'cause that wire was awful rusty."

Doug's face was already pale. "Are you sure you have to do that?" he asked.

The medic told him of the dangers of lockjaw and gangrene, and that if not treated properly, a future penidectomy might be required. "Sergeant, we absolutely need to flush out the injury with iodine and methiolate. This is only going to burn a little."

The medic pulled out the offending piece of wire spike, jabbed in the injection and dumped on the iodine and various other disinfectants while Doug howled and caterwauled.

Overall, the incident was good for team morale, in a black humor sort of way. We debated for hours about the best way to write up the Purple Heart (err, Purple *Shaft)* award recommendation, and all the while old Doug just sat there and fumed.

No matter what branch of the service, certain experiences are common to all enlisted soldiers. The hours are long, the duty can be filled with mind-numbing repetition, and small rewards sometimes seem precious enough to be worth a bit of risk.

GOING OUT THE BACK DOOR

By Don Collins

When I was stationed in Berlin during the early 1970's, there would occasionally be student demonstrations against the war. Interesting, isn't it? West German students, themselves living in close proximity to communist East Germany and Russia, violently protesting their ally and protectors' fight against communism half a world away.

While the protests usually didn't concern me one way or the other, one night one of them happened to take place on my night off, and I had no intention of spending my free time sitting in the barracks. I wanted to get drunk. I'd been working hard, and felt I deserved it.

I was living at the Anderson Barracks. My Plan A was to walk out the front gate, just as if nothing was happening. To my surprise, it worked! The guards just looked at me and let me go. I started walking down the street towards a quiet little German bar. I was actually within ten feet of the door when the O.D., a young 2nd lieutenant, pulled up in a jeep with two MP's. He chewed on my butt a little and ordered me back to the barracks. What was worse, he sat there and watched me go. Bummer!

Well, I wasn't going to let a little bad luck stop me. I knew there was a hole in the fence over by the NCO club. It was on a different side of the barracks than the main gate, where I knew the O.D. would still be watching like a hawk. I snuck through the fence and once again headed down the street—when who comes around the corner but the O.D.! This time I got his 1ˢᵗ class grade A premium butt-chew. He personally drove me back to the main gate and told me that if he caught me again I was going to spend the rest of the night in jail. Major bummer!

But that's one thing I know about life, you can't let the little setbacks get you down. Okay, I figured, this guy is watching the main gate, and he obviously knows about the hole in the fence…so, what's left? It came to me in a flash of inspiration—the M.P. Headquarters! I'd been over there a few weeks earlier to get a pistol permit, and while I was there I noticed that it had a door to the outside. This door was connected by a hall to a door going to the barracks, so that Germans could come in and file complaints. As I remembered it, the way it was laid out, the M.P. Desk Sergeant couldn't see the hall. When I'd first seen it, I'd simply thought it was a little odd; but now I saw it as my golden opportunity. I walked right through the M.P. Headquarters without anyone challenging me, walked right out the other side, and made a clean get-away!

I wasn't foolish enough to head for the same bar. That's the good thing about Germans, they do love their alcohol, and I found an excellent bar five or six blocks from the barracks. Once there, I proceeded to accomplish my objective for the evening. Some time later, fortified by my intake, I was actually looking for an M.P., hoping they would pick me up and take me back. But, naturally, you can never find one when you really need them. And the good news was, I didn't run into the O.D., either.

This experience is common to young soldiers throughout history. It happened thirty years ago to a young trooper who was a member of the ASA stationed in Southeast Asia.

THE BOY SOLDIER & THE PROSTITUTE

By Gary Lorentzen

When I arrived in Vietnam in the spring of 1969, I was only 18 years old. I'd joined the Army Security Agency when I was still 17, and I completed basic training the week of my 18th birthday. I had my 19th birthday at Phu Bai, and shortly thereafter was transferred to the 330th in Pleiku. I wasn't the most sexually experienced human being at the time, and Phu Bai hadn't afforded me much opportunity to change that. But Pleiku was a different story.

I resolved I was going to finally put an end to my status as a virgin, so on my first day off, I got together with three other guys and we went to Pleiku City. These guys didn't really know my objective, but we all were agreed we were going to find a *house* so we could enjoy some sexy fun. The place proved to be comfortable, clean and nicely decorated, but I wasn't particularly relaxed or focused on my environment, so it didn't matter much to me at the time.

The way it went, the Mama-san paraded the young women in front of us. Almost immediately, one caught my eye. Being the professional she was, the Mama-san noticed immediately. She grabbed my hand and pulled me to my feet.

"You cherry-boy," she said. "I know cherry-boy when I see. This girl do you good time. No problem. No sick. I see you like her."

145

She took me down a hallway, smiling and pulling me along. As we left, she gave a brief hand-signal, and the girl followed us. I kept looking back over my shoulder to make sure the right girl was following us. I will confess I had a mild anxiety attack when we reached the door to our room. I even resisted Mama San's patient tug for a moment, but then quickly gave in and followed her through the door.

Mama San spoke in Vietnamese to the girl I'd selected, and then handed her a key. The young girl gave me a shy smile and motioned that I was to follow her. We went together down another hall and stopped at a bedroom door. She unlocked it and beckoned me to enter.

By now I was very nervous, and yet I was determined to go through with it. I thought my girl was very beautiful, but I was afraid and anxious. *What if, for some unknown reason, I wouldn't be able to do it?* She seemed to understand. She was very kind and gentle, and calmed me down enough so that I was able to sit comfortably on the bed.

She had long, beautiful dark brown hair, translucent skin and a terrific, petite body. She slowly took her clothes off and sat naked, framed in the room window that looked out on an inner courtyard. Framed against the bright light of day, her silhouette was stunning. She turned to look at me. She didn't have to say anything. I knew it was my turn to take off my clothes. The truth is, I'd been so caught up in her beauty I hadn't thought about it until then. I unbuttoned my uniform shirt and undid the buckle on my belt. She stood up and walked over to me. I was struck again by the beautiful proportions of her body. One moment I had been lost in the perfection of her dark, luminous eyes and her oval face, and then her body was the only object in my field of vision.

She leaned over and kissed my lips, and the world stopped. At that moment, I was no longer worried about my performance. My mind disconnected and the age-old moves of natural biology took command. She was terrific. She knew what to do, and when, and where. I don't know how long the earth stood still; I only know that it did, for me.

But then, the job was done. Well done, but still, done. Being the professional she was, she jumped up, grabbed her clothes and walked out of the room. I lay back on the bed, staring at the ceiling. After a while, I dressed and walked back down the hall to the reception room. Mama-san was waiting for me. She scurried up to me, grabbed my sleeve and smiled a big, toothy grin.

"You no more cherry-boy, huh, G.I.?! That's good for you!" To avoid further embarrassment, I took out my wallet and handed her fifteen MPC and headed to the door.

Mama-san laughed, "You go now, G.I., but you come back, okay?" I nodded that I would. "You come back and bring friend, okay, G.I.?"

I walked out the door, walking through the tropical heat of the day. I sat on the steps, waiting for the others to come out. I took a deep breath and thought about my experience. It came to me in a flash that I hadn't worn a condom. I had a sudden panic attack. They always told us in basic training that we should piss after sex, and that would help reduce the risk of venereal disease. I jumped up and ran back into the house. I found a bathroom and took a leak, and then grabbed the soap and scrubbed the Little Man until I thought I was chaffing the skin. My heart was pounding and my hands were shaking. Cleaning up did ease my mind a little, but I was still nervous. What if I came down with the clap or the crabs, or even some Godless, unnamed, incurable syphilis?!

I heard the voices of my friends down the hall. They were talking to the Mama-san. I went back to the reception room as they were paying up, and we all left together. As we walked down the street, everybody was graphically describing his respective experiences. I couldn't figure out how to explain what I'd experienced without revealing that I'd been a virgin. I decided to smile and nod and not give out any more information that I had to.

In the end, there wasn't really any down-side to the experience. I didn't come down with any unseemly disease, and I did feel a glowing sense of joyful accomplishment, what I now recognize as an adolescent pride, a healthy inflation of my male ego. I was no longer a boy, I was a primordial man. Perhaps there are those who will think I had become stupid with delusions of grandeur and invulnerability, but in truth I had made my long-awaited passage from neuter child to male. In that moment, I enjoyed an archetypal fellowship in a male fraternity of sex and war, and I experienced feelings only a 19 year old soldier can feel. I was self-centered, penis-centered, and *That was okay, G.I.* I felt like a young Tarzan, and I was going to live forever.

And what of our young car thief, last seen earning a purple heart for being blown up in the back room of a Saigon bar? The ways of mischief and thievery die hard, and there seemed to be opportunities for economic advancement of this sort even in the military, even when one has a Top Secret Clearance and works as an electronic spy in the middle of a war zone. Apparently one of the better ways to survive a military conflict is, whenever possible, to keep your sense of humor.

THE DEUCE-AND-A-HALF AND THE HOOCH FRIDGE

By Jack Waer

It was 9 May, 1964. I woke up in my assigned corncrib at Davis Station with a hangover and the nagging thought that *today was a special day*. It came to me while performing my morning 5 S (shave, shit, shine, shower and shampoo). Today I was a civilian! My current re-enlistment was up! No one had checked my records. No one had asked me to re-up again. I was going to re-up anyway, but why not have some fun?

I threw on some civvies instead of a uniform and trudged over to the mess hall to have some breakfast. The 1st Sergeant looked up from his own plate of duck's eggs and roared, "God DAMN it, Waer, what the hell do you think you're doing?"

"Breakfast, sir," I said with a big smile.

"God DAMN it," he bellowed, "Get your ass in gear, get your uniform on, and GET TO WORK!"

"Ohhh," I said calmly, "You'd like me to pay for my breakfast because you realize that I've been a civilian since midnight."

"WHAT?!"

"Well, no," I continued, "I've got the money right here." My smile broadened, "Let me see…this must mean I'm no longer subject to the Uniform Code of Military Justice."

He gaped and his face got red and his eyes bugged from his head. I thought he was going to have a heart attack there and then, but he stormed out of the mess hall, instead. I figured I might have a little time so I got my tin plate and started heaping on the food. Nobody said much but everyone from the Mess Sergeant on down to the serving boys was grinning, wondering *What is Crazy Jack trying to pull off this time?* I was on my second cup of coffee and first cigarette after breakfast when our Commanding Officer (we called him The White Snake) came barging in with the 1st Sergeant tailing after him like a puppy dog. The White Snake had my 201 file with him.

He slammed it on the table in front of me as he struggled to speak, "God DAMN it Waer, why didn't you say something about this last week?"

"Nobody asked me, sir." I threw my hands up in a gesture of helplessness. "I thought it was your job over in the Orderly Room to keep up on things like that." I could see that both of them were worried that I was going to go to the Inspector General or something like that. *Verrry good, thinks I. Let's see if I can milk it for all it's worth.*

My comment had quieted down the White Snake. He gave me a calculating look, "What say you come over to the Orderly Room so we can talk this over."

"I'm sorry, Sir, but I can't do that right now."

"Why the hell not?" the 1st bellowed. The White Snake held him back from physically attacking me.

"Well, I haven't finished breakfast yet. But I'll be glad to join you in…" I glanced at my watch, "…say 20 minutes or so."

At about this time, the Mess Sergeant showed up with a separate rations sheet for me to sign. "Oh, for God's sake, give me that!" The White Snake snatched the sheet from my hand and signed it himself.

"Thank you for breakfast, Sir," I said.

True to my word, we reconvened in the Orderly Room a little later. We got down to some hard and serious bargaining. I got the next week off for an R&R in Thailand, an extra three days off from work when I got back, two cartons of Luckies, and four bottles of Old Granddad—and they came through with all of it! Still, I figured I needed something extra, something *to boot*, as the old masters of the sharp deal used to say. I made them call the hanger (the Security Restricted area where I worked) and tell them I wouldn't be there that day.

By then I could see they were both getting twitchy, so to their great relief I re-upped at about 0900 hours. The Company Clerk signed off on it, and we had a deal. Since I had the rest of the day off, I went over to the sign-out log and prepared to go to downtown Saigon for the day.

The White Snake sighed, "Would it be too much to ask for you to drop this off at MACV Headquarters on your way?"

"I'd be glad to do that, Sir" I replied, accepting a big brown envelope. With that, I was out the door and on my way. It never does you any good to hang around once a deal is struck. I've always believed you have to leave before they have second thoughts.

I did go downtown and managed to deliver the envelope. After that I went to Pop's Place on Nguyen Hue Street, across from the USO, for a water buffalo sandwich on a French roll. I'd finished my buffalo burger and was sipping my second *Ba Muoi Ba* when *Lo and behold!* I noticed a deuce-and-a-half pulling up to the USO. They parked on the street. An officer got out of the cab and six or seven G.I.s in uniform piled out of the back. I noted that the driver, even though he was an officer, foolishly did not put a chain or lock around the steering wheel! After all, we were in a war zone, and anything might happen. Something, I decided, probably would.

With great dignity and aplomb, I sauntered across the boulevard and peered into the truck. I was right—no chain or lock! And this is where the instincts from a misspent youth in Newark, New Jersey, took over. After all, a judge who gave me the choice of uniforms—army or jail, had shoe-horned me into the military in the first place.

I climbed into the cab, started the rascal up, put her in gear, and took off down Nguyen Hue, headed towards the river. I turned right at the Floating Restaurant and then noticed a 2nd Lieutenant's uniform hanging in the cab. There it was, fresh from the laundry. More possibilities! Technically speaking, you could say I was still a civilian, at least until my paperwork was processed, and so I didn't think of it as impersonating an officer.

Wondering what to do to exploit these new developments, I followed the river road until I came to a dock with a U.S. freighter moored along-side. There was a line of several trucks waiting to load up. Aha! Things were becoming clearer!

I pulled into the line, put on the officer's blouse and waited. When it was my turn, I pulled into position and was loaded with 12 crates that were about 4x4x10 feet in dimension. I calmly drove away toward the Cholon area, where I found a quiet place to park. Upon investigating the crates, I found they were Kelvinator refrigerators!

My, my, my! What is one to do with twelve refrigerators? I thought of something. I stopped at every military compound I could find and traded eleven of them for barter goods. I got six big boxes of frozen steaks (we had steak and eggs for breakfast), twenty cartons of brown jungle boots (they were no good; the soles fell off with regularity), one Villiers 125cc motorbike, twenty-five ration books, one stereo system and $1,200. Not a bad day's work.

I drove back to Davis Station with the one remaining fridge and my goodies. I sent the steaks to the mess hall, the boots to supply, the fridge to my hooch and the rest to me as compensation for my risk and hard work. What was I to do with the truck? A little OD and black paint from supply took care of the bumper markings, and the guys who worked in the hanger could all thank me for riding to work instead of walking!

All this, plus the goodies I got for re-upping! MAN, WHAT A DAY!

In military intelligence, as in the rest of the army, every soldier is assigned a weapon and is expected to be able to use it. So you had people, often myopic from birth and half-deaf from listening to covert chatter through a field of static who had to look sharp on foggy nights while listening for the faintest rustle in distant brushy shadows. It was often while on guard duty that the disparity of the two ways of life—that of the electronic spy and that of the warrior—was most apparent.

MANNING THE ROVING PATROL BUNKER

By Gene Richert

Guard duty was one of the real joys of the year I spent with the 8th RRU in Phu Bai, which is way north in South Vietnam, in fact just a few clicks south of the DMZ. With the exception of the occasional rocket attack, guard duty was the only brush I would get with the real war, that is, the war of blood and bullets where people died violently without warning. I loved the secure feeling it gave me to guard that lovely ammo dump, and the few hours I spent trying to sleep on sandbags were great training for future backpacking adventures once I got back to the World. Okay, so much for satire.

My 'normal' job in Vietnam was a couple of steps removed from *The Field*. I was a Radio Traffic Analyst—one who tried to figure out what enemy units were out there, where they were, and what they were doing, by analyzing what they said on the radio.

The troopers of the 8th were responsible for the thirteen bunkers on Echo Sector, as well as providing guard personnel for a roving patrol bunker that connected Echo with Foxtrot. Each bunker had six guys manning it, except for the Roving Patrol, which had nine.

The Roving Patrol bunker had to send a patrol out twice a night. This patrol was equipped with a PRC-25 radio, an M-79 grenade launcher and two M-14s. They had to make contact with the last bunker on E sector and the first bunker on F sector.

We had cut cards for who would go out on patrol first, and I lost. The patrol left without me, and those of us left settled down on top of the bunker. The other guys were Ted Twardowski and Jim Stald from Philly, and two Texans, Bill Stone and Gordy.

It was just about dark. Jim, Ted and Stoney were playing cards.

Jim suddenly said, "Quiet! I hear something in the wire!"

Each bunker was defended by several rows of either razor or barbed wire with empty tin cans strung on every few feet. Pebbles in the cans made them rattle if the wire was moved. The bunker's final line of defense, other than the men with rifles, was several claymore mines, shaped charges of explosive with imbedded shrapnel that we could fire from a remote area. One side of each claymore was clearly marked, THIS SIDE TOWARD ENEMY.

We all knew Jim could be pretty shaky, so we did our best to calm him down.

"Jim, it's nothing."

"Forget it, Jim."

"Naaa, nada."

But the reassuring words were barely out of our mouths when we all heard the cans rattling. Somebody was out there in the middle of the concertina wire, messing with our defense system. Maybe they were setting explosive charges. Maybe they were turning our own claymore mines around, pointing the shaped charges directly back at us!

That settled it; Jim charged the M-60, a light but effective machine gun, while the rest of us locked and loaded our M-14s.

Stoney shouted, "Halt! Who goes there!"

There was no answer. And here's where Vietnamese politics reared its ugly head. None of us wanted to risk an Article 15 for popping a hand flare, because unauthorized use of pyrotechnics could get us fined 1/3 of a month's wages through an Article 15; and yet we couldn't see who or what was in our wire. I cranked the field phone to get an authorization, but it didn't work. *Has anyone ever seen a field phone this side of the movies that actually worked?*

By now you've figured out that none of us were career patrol guards. By day, Gordy was a TA, a Traffic Analyst or 98C as they were numbered. They are tricky and resourceful fellows known for coming up with clever answers, and Gordy thought he'd come up with a solution. Our clever TA reasoned, Since our bunker was pretty much hidden from the command bunker by hills, why wouldn't an illumination grenade work just as well? He dove into the bunker and returned with a gray canister. He'd had this in basic training. He knew just what to do. He pulled the pin, prepared to throw, and threw the can in a short, graceful arc. We waited, and waited, but in vain. It was a dud.

Our brave 98C dove back into the bunker and came out with what looked like another illumination grenade. He threw another beautiful arc right into the source of the noises! We waited and finally there was a *Pop!* and our little hollow was filled with thick, white smoke. In the darkness and his haste, he had mistaken a WP Smoke grenade for an illumination grenade.

The smoke finally cleared, and it was none too soon, because at just about that time the Sergeant-of-the-Guard drove up in his deuce-and-a-half. We knew this sergeant. He was an 09B, a regular infantry sergeant who was being given a break from being in the field, and certainly not the sharpest spoon in the drawer.

"How's it going tonight, men?" he asked.

"Just fine, sir. Just fine," we all replied.

We were concerned that we might over-arouse the good sergeant's combat instincts. And there was the Article 15 to worry about.

Stony put on his best silver-tongued show. "All is exceptionally fine, sir. But would you please report that our field phone isn't working?"

This was an excellent strategy, as it gave the sergeant something to do. Chest puffed out, he was pleased to drive off on his new mission.

The next morning, as part of our Standard Operating Procedure, we checked out our claymores. Several of them had been turned around, pointing the business end in our direction. So there had been a VC or two out there. It was some comfort knowing that we'd at least scared the poor devils by lobbing what could have been deadly fragmentation grenades in their direction. That morning, somewhere in a liberated village in South Vietnam, there was a mamasan who was hard at work, laundering her sapper hubby's exceedingly soiled black pajamas.

Continuing the further adventures of the young car thief from New Jersey, we find out how he earned one of the most serious of his half dozen Purple Hearts, and how he found his way back to a relative form of sanity thereafter.

THE POW INTERROGATOR

By Jack Waer

I guess you could say I've done a lot of things in the little corner of the world called at various times Indo Chine, Indo China and Vietnam. I was actually in Dien Bien Phu as an American adviser when the French were still in Vietnam, and all told, I spent a total of 8 years, 10 months and 23 days in that country. Over that time, I'd been an Airborne Ranger and a Traffic Analyst in the ASA. I'd also been in MACVSOG, and then a POW interrogator.

When I first arrived in Vietnam, I was 17. When I came back the second time, I was 24. And by the time I became a POW Interrogator I was 32. Up until then, I'd received 5 Purple Hearts, though I don't want you to mistake this as saying I'm any kind of a hero. I'm lucky.

I remember one day in the spring of 1968; in three days I was going to celebrate my 33rd birthday. I had voluntarily extended to stay in Vietnam a few times, and my current extension was due to run out in five months. As we said back then, *149 days and a wakeup.* Something was different for me, and I'd made up my mind I would definitely leave, and I wasn't going to come back. I was a Staff Sergeant, and I'd just gotten word that I was going to make Sergeant First Class at the end of the month. With the completion of my service here, all my tickets were punched. I should have an easy assignment back in the Land of the Big PXD, or maybe I'd opt for a cushy Thailand tour. I wasn't quite sure what I'd do, but it was going to be good.

When I thought about it, one thing was clear; it was 1 Feb 1968, and there were three days left until I would be 33, and the local beer was called 33 Biere, or Ba Moui Ba in the native tongue. I figured it must be a good omen, and I resolved that before the end of the day I would have to get me some.

At that time I was a mobile interrogator. That meant that they would assign me anywhere the action was, anywhere that they were taking prisoners. I'd been sent 5 klicks west-northwest of Hue, which is the old capital of South Vietnam. This was in Central Vietnam, up near the DMZ. I'd just finished interrogating a captured Viet Cong on what we called the Essential Elements of Information (EEI). It should have been easy, but there was a problem; I found the answers the guy gave me to be very disturbing. The POW kept saying I was going to die today; I was going to be a victim of their Tet Offensive.

I didn't know anything about any big push. Nobody on the American side did, really. The VC had been threatening a Tet Offensive for years, and nothing had ever come of it. Still, there was a lot of activity going on...but, on the other hand, in this area there always was a lot of activity. I only had an hour with this guy from the time of his capture. After that, I had to forward him on to higher HQs for a more detailed interrogation. I did what I could, and then took the POW into Hue.

Usually a couple of GIs or MPs transport the prisoners, but this time they were short on vehicles and so they ordered me to go along. It was 0500 hours on a fine, clear and crisp morning. I was driving the jeep, with an MP beside me, and one directly behind me. The POW was next to him.

I was somewhat of an expert at acquiring jeeps. I'd found this one unattended several weeks before and claimed it as my own. I'd put new bumper markings on it, marking it as belonging to the 3rd Radio Research Unit (3rd RRU), a unit I'd previously served in and for which I retained a great fondness. When the MPs asked me what the 3rd RRU stood for, I told them it belonged to my parent unit, the 3rd Recon

Repatriation Unit. There appeared to be some doubt in their minds, and I made a mental note to repaint the bumper marking when I got to Hue. I remember thinking maybe I should mark it the 1st CRU, for Canteen Repair Unit. Military humor. You have to get your fun where you can find it over here. Maybe CRU was too obvious…I remember musing on perhaps some other designation just as we started over the bridge going into Hue proper. And then, I was thinking *Why am I flying?* And after that, there was nothing.

I opened my swollen eyes to a bright grayness. I couldn't move. I couldn't focus. I couldn't hear anything. The pain was unbelievable. My legs and my right arm wouldn't move. My neck and head wouldn't move, either. *Awwww shit, my luck had run out!*

After some experimentation, I found I could move my left arm a bit…but even that movement was restricted by the myriad of tubes sticking from it. By tentatively exploring with my left arm, I found out I was in a full body cast that encased my right arm, neck, torso and both legs. But it appeared, at least on my primary inspection, that I had all the requisite number of body parts.

I lay there for some time, and then, all of a sudden, there was an oriental nurse peering at me. Her lips were moving, and she was apparently talking to me—but I couldn't hear anything. Some guy in whites appeared and was checking my eyes and other vitals, or so it seemed.

It came over me with a rush—that POW was right! They had gotten me! Now the interrogator was the prisoner, and was going to be the interrogee! I had pushed my luck too far. Now I was the prisoner! It was too much, and I faded to black.

Days passed, and my hearing slowly got better. I was in morphine la la land most of the time.

And then one day a Chaplain walked in. "Good morning, son!" he chirped. "How are we feeling today?"

I didn't say anything but I thought *I don't know about you, but I feel like shit!* I wasn't going to tell him anything. Even in my drug-induced state, I knew who this was; it was some turncoat, some traitor working for the enemy!

"We have a little problem here," he continued. "We are 90% sure you are an American GI, but you had no identification or uniform when you were found. We need your name, rank, serial number and date of birth so we can notify your next of kin to tell them where you are."

"Where am I?" I managed to mumble.

"You're in Letterman Army Hospital, in the Presidio of San Francisco."

I wasn't buying any of it. After all, I knew all about this crap, I did it for a living. First they pretend to be your friend, and then they go for the information. I said, "I am a POW in Vietnam, and I refuse to give you any information of any type."

He had a great act. He seemed genuinely surprised, and when he persisted with his questions, I gave him the finger.

Several days passed, and then a full colonel appeared by my bedside. He gave me the same old story about where I was. I figured I'd have some fun with him. Well, Colonel, if I am at Letterman, I'll give you an address in San Francisco. From Letterman it should take less than a half hour to get there. You or one of your men go there and phone me and tell me what is there."

I used to drink at a bar called The Question Mark at 14?37 Haight Street. It was an actual address with a sign that said 14questionmark37. The Colonel seemed to take me seriously. He agreed to do as I asked. In about an hour, he came back with a phone and a young man in whites. He took his watch off and placed it on my chest and said, "What's the address?"

I replied, "14questionmark37 Haight Street. The fellow in whites went off, and the Colonel made himself comfortable in a chair by my bed. Twenty-two minutes later the phone rang. The Colonel picked it up and handed it to me.

"Hello?" I said.

"Hey! It's a bar called the Question Mark, and the sign in front says 14?37."

"Holy shit! What's the owner's name?"

"Harry Pepper. He's standing right here."

"Holy shit! Put him on!"

There was a pause and then a voice said, "Hello, this is Harry."

"Harry, do you remember a guy called 'Scooter'?"

"Yeah, I remember him. Wild sort of fuck."

"Harry, this is important: What did Scooter drink?"

"He was in the army and went to Vietnam."

"What did he drink?!"

"Jack Daniels on the rocks…"

"Holy shit!"

I was indeed in San Francisco. My jeep had been hit with a 122 rocket, and I was the only survivor. I had been medivac'd out and in a coma for 10 days! I had earned my 6th Purple Heart with an unbelievable 239 fractures and multiple wounds. I spent the next 17 months apologizing to everyone at Letterman, but the important thing was, I was home!

That long awaited event, coming back to 'The World', coming home to the United States, wasn't as many ASA troopers imagined it might be. The place had changed. Respect and civility were routinely replaced with taunts, jeering responses, scornful spitting and lofted balloons of pig's blood for soldiers who had gone to Vietnam. Those in military intelligence had a double burden— they knew more than most about the war, and were sworn to say less.

REQUIEM FOR A WAR

By John Klawitter

It was the early 1970's and Nixon's answer was *a-blowin' in the wind*, he wasn't going to lay a Lincoln on the American people, wasn't going to hang tough over the emancipation of Southeast Asia, a place crowded up with yellow-skinned folks who mostly couldn't speak English anyhow. Only nobody I knew seemed happy about his decision; half the people were angry because we were pulling out and the other half furious that it was taking so long.

I thought I knew more first-hand about it than most, but I learned to stay out of the arguments, which always seemed to turn into ugly yelling-matches. I'd been back from Nam since June of 65; I'd joined up and done my best and nearly gotten my head blown off for my trouble. In terms of the war effort, it seemed like my personal contribution had no effect at all, and I'd returned to the silence and jeers of an ungrateful nation…so I tried to stay disconnected, as if there was no reality there any more.

I was still a little shaky, even though my war was a thing of the past. I'd gone, I'd seen it, I'd come back with all my limbs intact. And then I got lucky. Like a dying grunt's fairytale, barely three months after my honorable discharge, I landed a job as a cub copywriter for the most prestigious ad agency in Chicago. Soon I was writing chatty breakfast cereal copy for Captain Kangaroo and creating happy little chocolate villages. I hadn't lasted, of course; I had great ideas, but I didn't know how to play the game, and sometimes I got serious at the wrong things, angry at the wrong things. I moved on to L.A., and then to Detroit, to write and produce TV commercials for cars, or as they say in Motor City, *to hawk the sheet metal*.

We were shooting mostly big corporate image spots for one of Detroit's Big Three to run on Sunday afternoon NFL football games, and I was flying weekly from Detroit to New York or L.A. The agency had a long-term lease on golden-toned, silver haired Leslie Nielson as their spokesman, and the car company's "Big Idea" was to come on like they were talking straight to the American people.

The outside creative source with the best reputation for shooting this sort of ad biz "true grit" was cameraman/director Haskell Wexler, who had made his reputation with the doc-style movie "Medium Cool", and, when he wasn't shooting movies, ran Dove Films out on the West Coast. I got a quote for a couple of spots, and, sure enough, the price was in the ballpark and Haskell was on for the job.

Now you may have heard of Haskell, or seen his name on the credits of some pretty decent movies. He's still around, and he's a big Hollywood name with those in the know, but back then he was a film maker about as new out of Chicago as I was. The difference was, he'd made a big wave with his quasi-documentary, "Medium Cool", a movie he'd reportedly shot with money inherited from the family shoe factory, while I had been dismissed from the clubby Chicago ad circles for moonlight-producing a political documentary called "Scene:Politic" that earned me an EMMY award and very little else. "Medium Cool" had spawned a whole wave of "realistic filmmakers", and Haskell had a little stage in old Hollywood on Highland near Melrose where, in between movie assignments, he did commercials under the Dove label.

I had heard Haskell had a lot of political liberals for friends, and that he was known to be difficult as a movie director, but he was supposed to be

terrific on commercials (where there was little enough of social consequence to argue about). The *Sheet Metal People* didn't have any problems
working with him, and everybody in the office was looking forward to the
shoot.

It was an early afternoon in February, a terrific Southern California
winter day with blue skies and just enough breeze to take the cut off the
hot sunlight. There was ankle deep slush in Detroit, but I was in L.A. for
at least another week. I was in a great mood as I swung my rented cherry
red Boss Mustang convertible into Dove's small parking lot.

Hallelujah! I couldn't believe my good luck. The lot was swarming with
beautiful women, dozens of all-American beauties, great legs, great faces,
great bodies stuffed in tight shorts and t-shirts, and they parted in smiling
flocks as I gunned the big V-8 into the vacant spot marked CLIENT. It
was a cattle-call for a soft drink spot, and I was ecstatic. *This was the REAL
Hollywood!* I'd been directing a few of the less expensive stand-up commercials for Ford myself; thanks to my old friend Arthur Pierson, I'd
joined the Director's Guild, and, though I was exiled to a distant Detroit
outpost, I sometimes even dared to think of myself as a
Hollywood-Guy-On-The-Way-Up.

But now, as I strutted past the girls in my self-appointed roll of
Hollywood V.I.P., in my mind the very picture of a young, macho-bullshit
director, I somehow missed a step as I was reaching for the door handle to
go into the Dove Films lobby.

I was off-balance and red-faced, and at that same moment somebody
pushed open the door from inside, and I was looking squarely into the
face of the ugliest woman I had ever seen…if not the very ugliest, at least,
one of the most studiously homely. Worse, it was somebody I knew, one of
the girls my Assistant Director had hired as a go-fur on one of my little
shoots. And worse yet, she had to make a big scene. She cried out, "Why,
DAR-ling!", threw out her arms and hugged me, planting a big ripe
smooch on my lips.

She was one of those surviving holdover renegades from the 60's, a discarded love-child. Up close like that, she didn't look any better than she had from a few feet away. Her hair was straight and unwashed, and chopped off in a ragged line somewhere down around her waist. Her teeth were chipped and stained, and her breath smelled of mentholated Kools, Maoi Wowie and garlic.

As a firm rule, I hated being kissed by anybody, even my wife, in public. I just don't like it, it's a hangover from when I was a kid and the aunts used to come gushing around. I staggered out of Ms. Homely's grasp, made what social remarks I could, and got inside fast.

On the other side of the door, I rubbed my sleeve across my mouth, shook my head and looked around. That wasn't real, this was. The lobby was overflowing with pretty girls. *What a job these Hollywood Moguls had!* Spirits reviving, I started down the hall. Jim, the head writer, poked his head out of a doorway and waved a handful of typewritten pages, "Client Approval!"

I grinned. It looked like the final hurtle had been jumped, we had the absolute green light to do the spots. Jim whooped joyfully, "And I've made reservations at Musso Franks for tonight!"

It was an agency ritual, when we got a big approval or finished a batch of spots we all gathered around a noisy, crowded table at Musso Franks for hot sourdough bread, steamed clams and many rounds of Heinekens beer. I raised my hands to the imaginary god of advertising creatives and sang out happily, "Troi, Dut, Nuoc, Oiii!", an old Vietnamese phrase which loosely translated means, "Sky, Earth, Water, Everything!"

Haskell stuck his head out of one of the other offices to see what the noise was all about. He had a lean, aesthetic look and a deceptively mild manner, "What on earth was that?"

"Vietnamese," I said, wondering why I had blurted that out in the first place.

Haskell perked up right away, "You speak Vietnamese?"

"Well, I used to. Forty-seven weeks at the Defense Language Institute in Monterey and a year in Saigon. I guess I learned something."

Haskell motioned to the people in the room to wait for him, and took me by the arm, walking a little ways down the hall to where we could talk alone, "Beautiful! What a coincidence! Look, you've got to come and see this film tonight."

I had only met Haskell a few days before, but the guy was an established Hollywood person, and I was flattered, *Hell, I could have steamers any time* "Well, sure", I said, "what kind of film?"

"Documentary on Vietnam. Beautiful footage. Shot by some Scandinavians. You'll love it."

I had momentary misgivings. It had been years since I'd been in Vietnam. I hadn't spoken a word of Vietnamese in all that time, "I won't be asked to translate or anything, will I?"

Haskell shook his head. "No, of course not. You've been to Vietnam, and I'd just like to get your opinion on the film. It's got a Scandinavian narration track, but we've got a translator coming to handle it." He gave me a conspiratorial wink, "And I want you to meet some special friends of mine…Deal?"

I took his extended hand, "Deal."

That evening, I pulled the Boss Mustang into a parking spot on the street as close as I could get to USC, glad for once that it was just a rented car. The neighborhood didn't look too safe to me, with graffiti scrawled on every available wall and a lot of what I took for gang kids loitering around, looking at the Mustang like it was a jeweled treasure ready for pillage. Haskell had drawn me a map of how to get to the cinema department, and I had no trouble walking the few blocks to get there.

The room was fairly small, and stuffy. Ten or fifteen scruffy film students sat around a long table on which rested a projector. A white screen was set up across the room. The kids mostly had hair down to their jackets, and beards serious as they could grow them. The preferred garment seemed to be faded army fatigues. I knew how hot and uncomfortable fatigues were; it was stuff I hadn't worn since the day I got out of the service. But I guessed they didn't care about that; it was polemics before personal comfort. I wasn't surprised to see most of them wore the "V for Victory" anti-war buttons and neck chain pendants with the drooping triangle peace symbol. One of them had a battered stars-and-stripes sewed on to the butt of his ragged jeans. Nobody was impressed by my designer suit or wide tie.

More students trickled in while I was being introduced, until the place was packed four deep back to the walls. My face flushed when Haskell made up a couple lies about what a great interpreter, how fluent in Vietnamese and what an expert on the war I was, and the worried note crept back in my mind. I didn't see anybody around that looked like a European interpreter.

The film was all set up on a dual projection system that I recognized as 16 millimeter interlock, a system that's uncommon in the advertising business, but is used by documentary filmmakers and students because 16 is cheaper than 35, and because you can show a picture around to try and sell it without taking it back to the lab for added expense of a finished answer print.

Everything seemed like it was set to go, but they were waiting for something else. Fifteen minutes went by, and we all just sat there. And then the door opened and there was a great flurry of welcomes and cheers-and in walked Tom Hayden and Jane Fonda! You know Jane from all the movies she's starred in, and it's old news about the controversy she stirred up over the Vietnam War. She had gone to Hanoi, been openly sympathetic to the North Vietnamese and the Viet Cong cause, and had allowed herself to be photographed in a flak helmet, peering knowingly up into the sky with a gun crew on the lookout for invading Gangster-American fighter-bombers, a picture with which Communist propagandists the world over had had a field day. At that time Tom Hayden was her husband, a famous radical himself, very influential in the anti-war movement.

I stared at Jane, and all I could think was that she was a lot shorter than I'd imagined. When you see a star like that on the screen, they use film magic to make them look bigger than life. I remembered hearing that Allan Ladd was short too, and they'd had him walk on wooden boxes for his role in the movie "Shane". I was wondering if Jane had done the same thing in "Barbarella", "They Shoot Horses Don't They" or any of the other films she'd starred in back before she began her anti-war push.

But then somebody snapped the lights off and the room full of scruffy students disappeared. The projector disappeared. Even Tom and Jane disappeared. To say it simply, I thought the film was WONDERFUL…but I didn't love it. For the first time in seven years I was back with the people I had tried so hard to help. I could smell the rich earth of the delta, the salty smell of gunpowder, feel again the muggy blasts of late spring heat and the thick rains of the wet, taste the pho and the nuoc man and the Beef Seven Ways, share again the fun and the tinny music and the bargirl laughter, hear the heavy saw of Brownings and the PAM of the M-1s, relive the stark moments when the flares drifted down and we all wondered if the sappers would get through this time…once again the heartaches, the hopes, the agony, the screams, the horror.

The interpreter didn't show up that night, but it wouldn't have mattered, because the Scandinavian narration track was missing anyway (if it ever existed). What they did have was a background track that was about 95% lip-sync Vietnamese. And the entire roomful of people turned to me, expecting me to tell them what was going on.

Part of me wanted to help, but it just wasn't possible. I had cauterized that part of my brain years ago, so I wouldn't go crazy. I felt numb, encased in ice. The students all wanted to know, *What are the Vietnamese saying, saying, saying…?* I just shook my head, my tongue frozen, brain frozen, emotions frozen.

It wasn't an empathetic time in America; there was no way those people could understand what was going on inside my head, and no way I could tell them. Pretty soon I was getting dirty looks, the students figuring out that I was CIA or some other government spy dropped in their midst. I wondered what they would do if they found out I'd been in the top secret National Security Agency, or that I'd had a Top Secret Codeword clearance?

It was ironic, in a way. We all were paranoid in those times. When I'd gotten out of the service, they made me sign papers saying I would forget everything I'd seen or heard, "in the interest of National Security". But I signed somebody else's name with the wrong hand, and I didn't forget…and on long, sleepless nights had penned lots of it in a messy, stream-of-consciousness novel that I'd unsuccessfully peddled all over New York and Hollywood. After I started writing about some of that *spy crap* and sending the manuscripts around, I was sure MY phone was tapped. I walked around actually waiting for a bullet in the shoulder blades. Nuts, huh? But at the time it seemed perfectly normal, just as logical as the angry stares I was getting from these college radicals.

I didn't care. The Scandinavian camera crew had concentrated on the haunting beauty of Vietnam, the lushness of the countryside, the primitive grandeur of the hamlet village society, the open friendliness on the peasant faces, the political purity of the Viet Cong in the liberated zones…all contrasted with the ugliness of the Invader-Gangsters, their rusty tanks, their false and foreign ways, the unfairness of their metallic might and rain of bombs against the native integrity-and yet the native strength would win out, for right was on their side. The political slant of the film angered me, but visually, the footage stunned me into quiet and forced me to examine images and ideas I'd tried to forget, to look again at a people I'd tried to leave behind.

The picture flickered to an end. The lights came on, and Haskell was looking at me like I was a traitor, like I'd sold out my own country. Haskell turned to Tom and Jane, making his silent apologies. I suppose I should have stood on the table and shouted that they all didn't know shit, that I'd studied the whole thing, that I'd gone to Vietnam and seen what it really was like, that the Vietnamese were good people, great people, and that they deserved to be helped, to be saved from communist domination. But I couldn't. It wouldn't do any good at all.

There wasn't a single mind in that room open to anything that I might say. The entire, subtle web of propaganda half-truths, just as effective as anything I could say about a Ford or a Schlitz or a Marlboro, had me pinned like a bug on the wall. I was just another poisonous creature labeled Invader-Gangster. I saw clearly in that moment the connections extending from 1960, the first time I'd heard protestors use the terms when I was a student back at UCLA, through all the hundreds of times I'd translated those words in covert VC messages at the Puzzle Palace in D.C. and the White Shack in Saigon, to this little room right in the heart of one of America's greatest universities: *Day Quoc Xam Luac My, Invader-Gangster American. Colonialist Pig American. Nguoi My Sao, Ugly American. Number Ten, Ugly American.* Inside, I felt bitter and crushed. And, looking back now, I can see it was in that moment I was forced to admit we had lost the war. It didn't matter that Jane Fonda was an empty-headed actress; what mattered was that masses of Americans were foolish enough to follow her lead. For me, the deepest, saddest truth was that the Communists, in alliance with the old-line radicals, the new-wave liberals, the self-indulgent draft-dodgers and virulent war protestors in this country, were going to beat us and pull us down with propaganda. They were going to win with words what they couldn't take with blood or bombs.

Nobody said anything much when the film was finished. The meeting broke up quickly, everybody thinking about the possibilities of hidden cameras and microphones. Feeling like a Saigon leper in my own country, I made my way alone through the Watts streets, walking back to the Mustang. Maybe I could still catch a few last steamers down at Musso & Franks. A few young blacks were sitting on the hood talking their jive talk, but it looked like nobody had swiped anything, and so I got in and drove away.

Soldiers who live, work and play together in difficult times can form deep lifelong bonds. But the time comes for all enlisted men when their term is up and they are free to go back to their old life. This isn't always as easy or as joyful as it seems.

MY VIETNAM BUDDY, SEAN

By Gary Lorentzen

I was thinking back to my friendships in the ASA and the friends I made in Vietnam, and how important they were to me. I didn't realize it at the time, but the memory of those friends and their loss would stay with me as time passed and the years went on. When my tour was up and it was my time to separate from the military, I felt a void in my life. The adjustment from the combat mode to the civilian way was difficult, but somehow losing very close friends and buddies was even harder. I remember my last day in the army, and the week or so that followed, and I remember in particular my buddy, Sean.

For my last year in the army, I was stationed in Washington, D.C. That was in 1971, and it was a hard period of waiting for me. It seemed the closer I came to the date when I would get out of the army, the more slowly the months would change on the calendar. At least my friend Sean and I were going through the same thing together. We'd spent the last four years together, stationed in the same places both stateside and in Vietnam. But after we were together in D.C, our friendship seemed to become deeper, one of those friendships of a lifetime.

I knew Sean felt the same way. Looking back, we could see that our experiences together had cemented a strong bond. We lived together in an apartment in suburban Northern Virginia. We worked and played together as we had for nearly four years. This time, however, we were alone in our own place, not in a military barracks with seventy other guys. Instead of getting on each other's nerves, the relationship seemed smooth and natural. Sean felt as I did—comfortable enough to be completely himself in my presence. For us both it was like living with family. We tried not to look too far into the future, realizing that we would soon be separating and going our separate ways.

But the day finally arrived. It was January 21, 1972, and Sean and I received our separation papers on that same day. We reported to Fort Myers, Virginia, to process the paperwork and take our walk away from the military life. I found it appropriately symbolic that we should be released from the Army on the solar ingress into Aquarius. How young and full of energy, ambition and hope we were then! The so-called New Age was dawning. Although the nation had yet to put Vietnam behind it, Sean and I felt we had moved beyond our Vietnam experience. The future stretched in front of us, sure and vast as the sky and the Great Plains we would cross in the days that followed.

God, how impatient I was to be on our way!

"Sean, let's go!" I yelled down the hallway to where he was still grooming in the bathroom.

"Yeah, yeah! I'm done, I'm coming! What time is it?"

I looked at my watch, "We have twenty minutes."

Sean rushed out of the bathroom. He was freshly shaven, splashed with Brut and dressed exactly like me, in olive drab fatigues, perfectly bloused at the tops of our highly polished boots. It was to be our last day in uniform.

"Grab the paperwork and let's go!" Sean drawled in a Texas way, and gave me a broad grin. His happiness was brimming in his eyes. Seeing him, I didn't feel so anxious any more, though I knew we both felt a little unsure about our futures.

We drove in silence down Route 50 to Fort Myers, just listening to the radio and sharing our excitement. I don't remember what I was thinking back then. It was a day of wonder, the kind of day when words seem superfluous, when your only feeling is one of wide-eyed anticipation.

I was twenty-one and Sean was twenty-two. As we stood in line at the processing center, we started talking about some of our experiences in Vietnam. It made me feel older than my years. The image of us, two young, green men in the war seemed incongruous. It was unreal or at least improbable to us that we should have gone through all that we had and come out safe and unharmed on the other side. Still, these were the normal everyday experiences that soldiers experienced in Vietnam; the odd experience of having mama-sans to clean up for us like maids, the ear-splitting roar of jet fighters taking off from the airbases, the rumble and thunder of the 500 pound iron-bombs as the B-52's conducted their raids, the psychedelic sounds of choppers crescendo-ing and de-crescendo-ing in the distance, the tense but often uneventful nights on guard duty, and the distinguishable whistles of in-coming and out-going mortars and rockets. These were among the sights and sounds of Vietnam as we remembered them. And as we talked, they gave me a small anxiety attack, or maybe an attack of conscience.

I looked at Sean, struck by the sudden realization that we didn't belong in this uniform. We didn't believe in this war. We had gone to Vietnam and extended our tour there for our own personal reasons. Sean was an artistic type, and I had fantasies of becoming an actor. We both leaned to the left in our political views. I had to put it out of my head; the contradictions were too difficult for me to even try to sort out at that moment.

"God, Sean, why did we do it? I mean, look at us! What were we thinking? Here we are, standing in our uniforms, waiting for them to let us out. We both volunteered to go over there." I stared at Sean in amazement. "Volunteered," I repeated. "What were we thinking?"

Sean smiled and shrugged. "Why do we do anything?" he replied. He was, as usual, unperturbed and unflappable. "It was the right thing at the right time, I guess…"

"But we both *hate* the war. We both hated Johnson, and we both hate Nixon."

Sean saw the problem. "So, why did we ask to go?"

"You know, I don't remember."

"I think it's because we were addicted to the adrenaline rush; at least, I think that's why we put in for another tour."

"You think?" I said slowly, rolling it over in my mind.

"Could be more. Maybe we have this ego problem that demanded we get involved in this historical event."

"What, we couldn't let them do the war without us?"

"Maybe…and maybe we weren't aware enough of the situation at the outset to take a moral stand."

Sean was at least partially right. For myself, my entry into the military was an attempt to resolve some of my personal problems. I felt that, in many ways, I had succeeded, though time would tell I hadn't resolved them all.

Sean smiled again, looking on the bright side. "In a way, we were lucky enough to have a war to run away to."

"Not a circus, but a real war, to break us out of the cocoon of childhood."

"Right," he agreed. "A war where we could escape social conformity and family expectations…and maybe find out what we were truly made of as men."

No question about it, our war adventures were archetypal and primal male experiences.

"I hate to admit it, Sean, but I'm going to miss it," I said wistfully.

"I know. Sometimes I miss it already."

Here we were, standing in line to get out of the army and I was falling into a blue funk. "There's a lot I hate about *The World*," I said. The World was this normal place of human activity. It paralleled our lives in Vietnam. While we were fighting, dying, being bored, going crazy, being frightened out of our skins and allowing ourselves the indulgences of living overseas, the people in The World were working their nine-to-five jobs, commuting to their suburban bungalows, living their standardized American lives, only vaguely aware of our reality over there. At that moment I clearly saw much of The World as superficial, neon, glitzy, shiny, cellophane-wrapped and television-soaped. I hated what I saw. I wanted to shake that world until it woke up and saw what I saw, the things that were really happening in the larger real world.

"You hate *The World,* huh?" Sean repeated with a half-smile. "You mean the whole world or just the world outside of the army?" He knew what I meant, he was just making conversation.

"Well, if I hated the whole world, I'd have to hate myself..."

"If you hate just the world outside the army, you might as well re-enlist right away."

"Okay," I admitted, "I don't really hate myself that much, and I can't possibly even think of re-enlisting."

"Then...?"

"I guess I was being a bit dramatic."

"Don't worry, Gary. We'll get used to The World again. It just takes time." I took comfort in Sean's reassurance. I could see he was concerned about me.

"I suppose..." I said, still not fully convinced I would make a smooth transition back to civilian life. "I'm just not sure that's a good thing, getting used to The World."

"Just think, my friend," Sean continued. "One moment we're in uniform, saluting, putting up with silly inspections and the rest of the bullshit—and real soon now we'll be free to think as individuals!"

"No more worries about where our weapon is."

"No more worries about saluting the next officer who comes along."

"God, it's a whole new life!" I smiled, thinking over the possibilities. Still, I was feeling a tinge of the old discomfort and anxiety. The army certainly takes care of you, and after a while you can come to depend on it.

Sean grinned, raised his fist in the air and looked down. It always made me smile when he struck the Black Power pose. Feeling the way we did about so many things, we identified strongly with the oppressed. We'd adopted that symbol as our own statement of resilience and resistance. We had resolved that we would not allow ourselves to be absorbed into the military mind. That simple gesture did something for us both. We stood quietly in line, making our way through the rest of the bureaucratic process. Every once in a while we'd make eye contact, smile briefly, nod and raise a silent fist over our heads. The medical exams were the last part. After that, we signed our final papers and became civilians.

We had made plans, and now was the time for them. Everything was packed. It wasn't much; it all fit into the front trunk of Sean's new, blue Volkswagen bug. We had tickets for a rock concert scheduled at William and Mary College. Traffic was the headliner, with J.J. Cale and Redbone. I remember it to this day, how Redbone stole the show in the smoky, Frisbee-filled air. After the concert, we climbed into Sean's VW and headed west.

It was after midnight. We were high on marijuana, rock music and our new freedom. The world was starry bright and my mind felt free and open. I fell into sync with the vibration of the car, curled up peacefully on my seat. Security and comfort spread through my limbs in the same way that anger and fear had so many times over the previous four years.

I looked over at Sean. He was staring through the windshield into the night, watching the road ahead as he drove. The shadows of his nose, chin and his gentle eyes contrasted sharply with the brightness of the headlights from the oncoming traffic. The stark black-and-white image etched itself in my feelings, and a strong wave of emotion began to well up inside of me.

I felt the need to tell Sean how much I cared about our friendship, and how much our experiences together meant to me. But such words wouldn't form on my lips. Sean's voice finally broke the silence, "Here, you want one of these?"

He was holding something in his hand.

"What is it?" I asked, leaning forward to get a better look.

"A Christmas tree."

"I don't get it."

"Amphetamines. The medic at Fort Myers gave me a few as a going-away present when I got my physical. It's green-and-white. That's why they call it a Christmas tree."

"Perfect," I said, and I meant it. I didn't want to sleep, anyway. We were hurling through the night, speeding further and further away from a painful past and breaking through to a wide-open future. I didn't want to miss a thing.

I knew Sean felt the same way. We both wanted to explore our new freedom, yet we were both slightly unnerved by our sense of being cast adrift in The World. It was oddly pervasive; the army takes over so much of your life that now the sense of being out of it was thick and tangible. We'd become accustomed to our complete envelopment in the military matrix, being told where to go and what to do. We were used to living in that very ordered world. And now we'd been suddenly released into a world where any order to our lives had to come from within. On the one hand, we wanted to escape from the military, but we still keenly felt the anxiety of the panoramic openness of the outside world.

The effect of the amphetamines began to take hold, and it seemed as if the speed of the drug came to match the momentum of the speeding car, dissolving the physical and mental barriers between us. In a moment of clarity I realized that Sean had been feeling as emotional and confused as I had, but neither of us could really express what we were feeling. Now, with the barriers gone, the atmosphere changed. We talked, we laughed, and we explored the universe within each other as we wrapped ribbons of the highway around our steel-belted radials.

We finally pulled into a truck stop somewhere in West Virginia. Everything seemed fine and funny at the same time. We laughed at ourselves for feeling uncomfortable eating breakfast alongside leather-faced truckers with Southern accents. We cracked suggestive jokes as the waitresses, women dressed in crisp pastel country-western outfits, their helmets of freshly sprayed hair piled in high swirls engineered with bobby pins. We created a Marx Brothers' dialogue in a Southern accent. We grinned, stared at everything, we got back in Sean's car and continued our journey westward.

Sean said he wanted to visit his family in Mineral Wells, Texas. I'd applied to college in Olympia, Washington, and I needed to arrive there sooner or later. But I wasn't worried about it. In those moments, for me, time had ceased to exist. I moved on the impulse of the moment, with no thought of limitations or responsibility.

"Hey," Sean said, "Let's go to Markham, Texas, and visit Jim Polk."

That seemed like a good idea. "Why not? Do you know where it is?"

"Somewhere down the coast, outside of Houston."

Jim had gotten out just before Christmas. We figured he'd be home. We both agreed he'd been one of the more intelligent guys we'd met in the army.

"I had some really interesting conversations with him," Sean said.

"Me too. A pretty smart guy, but he got kind of flaky there towards the end."

"You mean the drugs?"

"Yeah. I think the army got to him there at the end."

"Started feeling the pressure," Sean agreed. "Crazy and intelligent went hand in hand for a lot of the guys."

"Okay, let's go," I said. So we headed southwest, towards the Texas coast. As dawn broke through behind us, the rays of the sun seemed to give us energy. Our speeding blue German machine purred on. West Virginia sped by, replaced by the rolling hills of Kentucky and Tennessee. The Mississippi flatlands disappeared into Louisiana, and then we were crossing East Texas. Finally Houston appeared, an urban sprawl across the flatness of the Coastal Plains. We knew Markham wasn't far.

It turned out to be a quiet, musty little town outside of Bay City. There didn't seem to be much in the way of prosperity. Sean had the address, and we soon pulled into a dirt driveway. I could see a small house that was covered with green tarpaper. It could have been a scene from the Great Depression, say from the year 1935. I had the impression that nothing had changed in a long, long time.

And then, there he was! Jim came out from behind the little house. When he saw us, he walked toward the car. His face clearly indicated he had no idea who we were or why we were there. But once he recognized us, he smiled and picked up his pace, walking quickly across the overgrown yard.

Sean and I stayed in the car. We'd looked forward to spending some time with Jim, but we were stunned by his family's apparent poverty. That's the thing about the army; you meet folks from all walks of life, and you sometimes don't have much of an idea of their background.

Jim leaned his arms against the open window on the driver's side of the bug. "I can't believe it," he exclaimed in his Texas drawl. "You guys lost, or what?"

"Naw," Sean replied. "Just heading home. Thought we'd stop by and say 'hello'."

"Well, you sure surprised me," Jim said with a smile. "So, what's up? What are y'all going to do now that you're out?"

I shrugged, "Go back to school, I guess. Have to do something with my life. How about yourself?"

"Make a life here," Jim answered, gesturing with his head to indicate the house and the town beyond. "It ain't much, I guess, but it's home, y'know?" From his serious expression it was obvious he'd been thinking a lot about it. "I'll find work in Bay City...or something." He paused again, "You goin' back home, Sean?"

"Well, just to visit, I think. I'm not sure where I'll end up. For sure, not Texas." His face lit in a broad grin.

Jim nodded his head, turned and exhaled so we could hear it. The conversation came to an abrupt end. Jim looked back at us, "Why don't y'all come on in. I'll gitcha a beer."

I could see Sean didn't want to get out of the car, and I know I didn't. It seemed to us like the hopelessness of the place might be infectious. We just wanted to be on our way.

"Uhh, thanks," I said, "but I think we have to split."

Sean chimed in, "We still have to make it up to Mineral Wells. Got to see the family, you know."

"Yeah," Jim agreed. "That's a stretch of road ahead of you." He continued struggling for words. Nothing came, and he finally slapped the doorframe a light tap, "It was good to see y'all…take care, huh?"

"Yeah, sure," Sean said. "You, too. Sorry we can't stay longer."

I sat in silence. I didn't know of anything I could add. Jim out of the army wasn't anything like I'd imagined he might be.

He stepped back from the car. "Thanks for stopping by," he said. "I gotta go pick up my Mom down at the post office. Good to see y'all. Y'all are crazy motherfuckers to drive all the way down here just to say hello!"

I just smiled and nodded my head in Jim's direction. He turned and disappeared into the little green house. Sean hit the ignition and we pulled out of the dirt driveway. We were quiet for some time as we headed out of town.

"What do you make of that?" Sean finally asked.

"I felt we were intruding."

"Me, too. You know, in his own element Jim seemed kind-of simple, maybe even sedate. That's not the way I remember him.

"No. In the army he seemed vibrant, with that sense of humor always going."

"And intelligent."

"Yet here he is telling us all that is in the past and now what he wants is to live a simple, uncomplicated, church-on-Sunday life in his small Texas town.

Sean shook his head, "You know, he has ten brothers and sisters."

"No! All living in that little shack?"

"Yep. Plus a mother and father."

I felt sad. Looking out the window, the local scenery and the flat lands reminded me of the Mekong Delta. We passed by shanties and old, run-down houses. Not that I was above that sort of life—as a child, I'd lived in similar circumstances in the rural Midwest. It was life in the margins, living a shabby life in a place that should have been rich and prosperous. In that moment of insight, I saw the landscape as an emblem of the moral poverty and injustice of the war, and of America itself, The World with all its contradictions. Jim wanted to stay there for much the same reasons Sean and I had been tempted to stay in the army. It was safe, it was something we knew. Even if there was no real comfort or ease, one got used to the continual struggle to survive. And thinking such thoughts, I was buoyed by a new awareness of my own independence. I felt exhilarated and focused. I wasn't going to stay in the margins, I was going to live in the mainstream of society.

I looked over at Sean. I could see he was sharing some of the same thoughts and feelings. *What of Sean and me?* A flood of memories filled me. I didn't want to lose my friendship with Sean. I wanted to reach out and hold him. For a time, while in the military, I had learned to hate very strongly. Now feelings of love and affection were breaking through the barren ground and pushing up to make themselves known. I had wanted this emotional breakthrough, but now I was panicking.

Sean seemed to be struggling with his feelings, and neither of us spoke. We couldn't talk about it; we couldn't let out our feelings. We were bonded together, yet our relationship was so frightening to us that we couldn't express our mutual respect and affection.

Macho grew in the land. The Texas sky fell over us, and we grew hard against the emerging desert. I had to face it; soon Sean and I would part. And yet we couldn't tell each other that it mattered or that we cared. In a way, we'd sped through a sort-of sound barrier from Vietnam to the States—and the concussion had shattered our link. We went along with the flow. We fled to our adolescent ways. We lost each other somewhere in the wastelands of West Texas.

"I think I'll go back to D.C.," he said, breaking a long silence. "I like it there. I'll find a place in Virginia and get a job."

"Well…" I replied, "I guess we should figure out where we're going next."

"I do want to see my parents. You can come with me, or whatever you'd like…"

I thought about it for a while. It was tempting to go on with him to Mineral Wells, but it seemed to me that would just be prolonging the inevitable. I needed to make this separation a clean break. I decided we both needed a simple, matter-of-fact, unemotional, everyday, see-ya-later. I took a deep breath, let it out and said, "Maybe I'll just catch the bus to Olympia. I need to get there soon, anyway. I guess I really should get my life squared away before I start college in March."

Sean didn't say anything for a while, but I could see he was thinking about it. "I can drop you off at the bus station in Fort Worth. For me, it's a straight shot home from there."

"Works for me," I said.

We continued in silence. The closer we came to Fort Worth, the more depressed I became. Once we were in the city, I started gathering my few things from the back seat. We weren't talking. Sean had the radio tuned to music. It was better that way; a good way to avoid any real interaction.

We pulled into the bus station parking lot, and I crawled out of the little car. Sean pulled open the hood of the front trunk and I gathered my things.

"There," I said. "Got it all."

Our goodbye was appropriately cool. There was a stiff handshake and a protective guffaw, and the mandatory promise to write, and then a final take-care. I felt miserable. I knew then it was all coming to an end.

I bought my ticket and we walked together to the parked bus. We stood there, not saying anything and not looking at each other. Sean was fidgeting slightly, hands in his front pockets. The driver began taking tickets and helping passengers up the steps into the bus. We moved aside, waiting until the last possible moment for that final goodbye. I was trying so hard not to cry that I couldn't speak.

The last person boarded, and Sean still wouldn't look up. His fists were clenched in his pockets. But there was nothing either of us could do. It was time to go. I started walking toward the door of the bus. Sean remained silent. I stopped. I couldn't let it go like this. I turned around and strode to him. I put my things on the ground and put my hand out to shake his hand, one last goodbye. "I'm going to miss you," I said in a near whisper. "You know that."

His eyes began to tear and his lower lip quivered. He placed his hand over mine and nodded, still saying nothing. It seemed that if he would say anything, raw emotion would take over and he would lose control. I dropped my hand, picked up my things and walked back to the bus. I looked briefly over my shoulder as I climbed up the steps. Sean was standing there, his grief obvious, just staring at me. I nodded my head in his direction, one simple nod, and disappeared into the bus.

Finding a seat was easier than fighting back the sense of total isolation and loss that I felt. The bus lurched forward. I looked out the dirty glass of the Trailways bus. The last I saw of Sean, he was leaning in a typical pose against his VW, which by this time was covered in Texas dirt. He raised a silent fist in the air and hung his head. I did the same. The bus pulled away in slow motion, and I closed my eyes, hoping to shut out The World.

I woke sometime later. The hum of the engine had lulled most of the passengers into an uncomfortable sleep. It was the middle of the night. I stared out the window, trying in vain to make something out of the terrain in the inky night. I leaned back and closed my eyes, remembering how Sean looked as he'd driven through the night across West Virginia. I shook off my sadness and fell back asleep. I knew that when I awoke it would be a new day, the start of a new time for both of us. The army had been the backdrop for our friendship, but without the war, we had chosen different directions. Sean was heading east, and I was heading west. We'd been together a long time, but now our paths had parted.

Two days later, I stepped off the bus into a cool drizzle. I was in the Pacific Northwest. The wet pavement reflected the silver sky, the reflection serving as a mirror. I felt again the harsh and powerful memories of Vietnam stirring inside me, and realized how much Sean had done for me.

He had humanized me in an inhuman situation. Whether we saw each other again or not, he would always be my brother.

And I realized one more thing—the war was finally over for me. It was February 1972. The sun was in Aquarius. I was home and I was free.

So in the end you can say there are those who went to Vietnam and those who didn't. There are those from both sides—who went and who didn't—who would rather forget all about it. And there are those from both sides who can't forget.

TEDDY POST'S WAR

By John Klawitter

He walks with a limp and an ornate cane, and when he's been on his feet all day you can see the pain in his eyes. But you don't say anything—nobody on the set dares say anything—because this is the same Ted Post who nearly lost his leg on a beach in Italy in World War II.

They dressed him for pre-op, which means they swabbed him down with alcohol in the big olive drab canvas tent where they were hacking off maimed limbs. When the saw-bones bent over to have a look at his face, to see if this one might survive the operation or not be worth the time, Teddy grabbed his dog tags, staring hard at the name stamped there.

"If you cut off my leg," he said grimly to the man he'd pulled close to his lips, "I'll spend the rest of my life until I find you. And then I'll hack your leg off."

"But you'll die if we don't," the doctor said, prying his dog-tags from Teddy's fingers and pulling back to as safer distance.

"I'd rather be dead. It's my choice. You do it my way."

"But the bones are all crushed," the doctor begged.

"I'll just be a little shorter on that side," Teddy said.

That's the kind of guy he is. Legendary Teddy Post. He's a Hollywood legend, too, a director whose list of television and movie credits spans four generations. What director worked with Clint Eastwood on both Hang

'Em High and Magnum Force? What director did both the pilot show for Perry Mason and the pilot for Cagney & Lacey? What director has done Gunsmoke, The Fred Astaire Show, Twilight Zone, Peyton Place, and Columbo? Teddy Post, of course.

Though I'm mostly known as a writer, I'm also a member of the Director's Guild of America. When I heard Teddy was teaching a Master Director's Class, I called down to see if I could get in. The course was limited to 12, "by invitation only", and was already filled. But at the last minute they called me back—somebody had dropped out and I was in.

This was in the spring of 1985. I'd just left (been booted from) my big-time job at Disney Studios, and so I had plenty of time. There would be 8 sessions in all, 4 hours every Saturday morning for two months. Over that span each of us would be expected to direct at least two dramatic pieces of 5 to 10 minutes in length, pieces that had two or more actors. I was working on a novel I called Lemonlips, a prequel to my novel Crazyhead that ended up being published by Random House. Lemonlips was loosely based on my own experiences in the army, a story about four young Americans who join the army, get into military intelligence and end up in Vietnam. I thought maybe I'd adapt some of the scenes I'd written to screenplay format and try them out on the class.

I knew Teddy had directed Go Tell The Spartans, one of the few Vietnam War motion pictures that had been produced up to that time. I went out and rented it, and for me it played like a lot of anti-war message movies I'd seen somewhere else before. In fact, it seemed more stereotypical than most. You had your stiff and dumb officer types, your sacrificial grunt-lambs, your distant foreign war that nobody understands, your ugly Americans kicking the natives around in a dumb-assed way, and your 'sensitive' type writer-hero—the scribe—who is aware and sensitive to it all in some superior knowing way. Of course, there is a certain universality to all warfare, and this becomes particularly noticeable when Hollywood throws it up on the silver screen in a diatribe: the blood and guts, the madness, the wrong people in charge, guns and killing are evil, the wrong people always die, and the Greek Chorus wails to let us know it.

Anyway, I'd been in the service and I'd been to Vietnam, and I'd been amazed and dumbfounded by what I saw and experienced. I'd seen insubordination beyond all belief, astounding greed, cruelty, stupidity on a grand scale and petty behavior...as well as occasional individual acts of kindness, sacrifice and heroism. I didn't know if my own writing was minor-key Hemingway or pulp-Heller, and I didn't care. I was just trying to get it down on paper.

The first time I tried one of my Vietnam scenes on the class, I did a little story where my four heroes, American cryptographer/linguists with top-secret clearances, are sent outside Saigon to work with Vietnamese Intelligence in a fairly unsecured area. The Americans spend their time fooling around and making fun of the war effort...but their mood changes once they realize their room is bugged.

I felt pretty solid about this scene because it was a recreation of something that had happened to me and several of my fellows back in 1964. But Teddy Post and my classmates jumped on my offering like vultures on dead meat. I could have understood if they would have attacked it based on my lack of experience directing dramatic material; after all, they seemed to tear apart everything everybody did, anyway. But what really depressed me was Teddy's reasoning in rejecting the piece. Not one word about my directing. Teddy kept saying, "Soldiers just don't act that way." It was all he would talk about.

I crawled back to my den and licked my wounds, trying to figure out what had gone wrong. I went back and ran Go Tell The Spartans. It was, at heart, an anti-war film, the story of what happens when the U.S. military high command foolishly insists on building a distant outpost in an area where the enemy has massive strength (and so was a parable about our foolish participation in the Southeast Asian conflict). In the film, the distant outpost is saved from instant annihilation by the presence of old war hand Bert Lancaster, who recognizes doom is coming and prepares the men for the fight of their lives (deaths). The characters are stereotypes: the gnarly officer who ruined his career by dropping his pants at the wrong time, the young sensitive writer-recruit, the smattering of drunks and dopers sure to "get theirs" when the shit comes raining down, the handful of inscrutable Vietnamese "friendlies" who either prove to be loyal or deceitful. Pondering that movie, I kept thinking *What the hell's wrong with MY stuff?!* Meanwhile, I didn't see any reason to just sit back, I was charging full tilt through Teddy's class.

It took a full week's effort to prep a scene, but like I said, I was "on hiatus", the Hollywood euphemism for "out of work." After selecting what I wanted to do, there was casting, blocking out the action and rehearsals. While my classmates tore each other's work apart with abandon, I noticed there were openings every week; maybe they just didn't have the time, or maybe these guys weren't so eager to get their own stuff up on the stage. I felt this was a big opportunity for me. I resolved to present a scene every time there was an opening. In a sense, I guess you could say I saved the class, because some weeks I was the only person who came with a scene ready to go. Without me there would have been nothing to tear apart.

That aside, I was learning. No matter how reluctantly, Teddy was showing me a hundred things; how to pull down an actor who was dominating the scene when he wasn't supposed to, how to shift the mood and the tempo, how to color the scene to make it say what you wanted. And my fellow-students were giving me lessons on how to accept criticism. A guy like me should be made to eat humble pie every once in a while. It makes me bearable in polite company.

I could handle all that, but Teddy still bothered me. He didn't like anything I did. He just sat there, frowning at the behavior of my four mad heroes. Was I being too presumptuous, performing my own stuff instead of a scene from *The Glass Menagerie* or *Death of a Salesman*? Did I have some terrible blind spot? Was my stuff just plain *bad*? I kept coming back to his first reaction to my first piece. *Soldiers just don't act that way,* he'd said.

For my final piece, I resolved to let out all the stops. I had written a scene that takes place in the so-called *Puzzle Palace,* the top-secret intelligence headquarters of the National Security Agency. I'd spent six months in that topsy-turvy place and thought I'd come up with a scene that said a lot about the way things were in the mid-60's. In my scene, three of our four heroes are goofing off, irreverent as ever, and in doing so, they manage to infuriate their superior officer. But there is more to the scene; there has been a tragic, yet amusing, incident. A drunken sergeant has fallen into a giant pulper used to dispose of the tons of top-secret waste paper that must be discarded every day. In fact, our quartet has had more than a little to do with that death, and have feelings about it ranging from a casual shrug to a haunting sense of guilt. Still, the army is the army, and the most pragmatic of our happy-go-lucky characters is going to use this incident to trick the officer into giving one of them his dream—an assignment in Vietnam.

My actors completed the scene without a hitch, even though it was somewhat longer than the previous ones I'd done. There was the usual stunned silence, and then hands shot up all over the room.

Beside Teddy, I had one other nemesis in the class, a ram-rod straight assistant director who said he'd been in Vietnam almost ten years. He claimed he'd started as an enlisted man and had risen in the ranks until he was field-promoted to an officer. This guy's hand shot up like a gun. Teddy ignored the others and nodded in his direction.

"The problem with this piece," the guy said, "is that I don't like any of these soldiers."

"I didn't know I had to direct them *likeable,*" I shot back.

"Well…believable, then. I was there, and I don't think they're believable."

"That's just your experience," I said. "You're pretty unbelievable yourself."

"How's that?" He looked genuinely puzzled.

"Well, you started as a private and ended up as a captain."

"What the hell difference does that make?"

"You're on the side of discipline and rigidity and The War Effort."

"That's dumb!"

"I don't think so. Suppose you'd started as a captain and had your ass busted to corporal, maybe just due to some unlucky moves you made, the wrong place at the wrong time, that sort of thing. I'm sure you might have a little more sympathy for my characters."

There was a titter from the class. The guy looked like he was going to say something else, but thought better of it and sat down.

Teddy cleared his throat from the back of the room. "I agree with the criticism. This is the same as the other war scenes you've done. These characters aren't believable."

This may have been the prestigious Director's Guild of America's Master Directorial Class, but I'd had it with my Master Director.

"You've got me, Teddy. I really don't know what the hell you're talking about!"

This was tantamount to Mutiny on the Bounty. Directors have the biggest egos in the world; a director on his set is the next thing to God Almighty, and Teddy treated his class like he was at the helm of Gone With The Wind.

His face got red and he lurched to his feet, waving the famous cane in my direction like an old M-1.

"You're not the only one who knows about Vietnam!!" he thundered.

"I didn't say I was. I said I don't know what you're getting at. You keep saying the same things, but I don't understand them."

But I'd launched Teddy on a rant, and he wasn't about to explain himself. "I know about war!" he shouted. "I was in World War II! What the hell do you think this cane is about?!"

"Yes, Teddy, you charged up the beach in that splendid great war. You told us."

"Oh, you think I don't know Vietnam? Is that what you think?! Young man, I directed what is arguably the best movie about Vietnam to this date! And I tell you, soldiers don't act the way yours do!! The way they mouthed off to that officer?! They'd have been in the brig—or shot!!"

It was suddenly clearer to me. "The soldiers you knew didn't act that way—not in YOUR war, Teddy. The war to save the world from Hitler. We didn't have that kind of motivation in the Nam War."

"The army doesn't change that much!"

"How do you know? You haven't been in the army in 40 years."

Teddy's voice was close to the top of its register, "You don't have to go to Vietnam to know about Vietnam."

"Well, it helps, Teddy."

My other nemesis, the assistant director, had been mulling my recent comments. Now he leapt to his feet, "Maybe your war experience *narrowed* your opinion rather than broadening it!"

"Right. The real thing makes you ignorant. Where do you come up with this stuff?"

"It could have…" he said in a low voice. But after that he sat down and shut his mouth.

It was my turn to rant. "All I know is, I went and saw for myself. It wasn't like Crane, it wasn't like Conrad, it wasn't like Hemingway, it wasn't like Heller—and it wasn't like Teddy Post!"

Teddy glowered at me "Well, tell us, Mr. Big Time War Expert, what was it like?" From the look on his face, I was glad we weren't taking the course for a grade.

"It was like my scenes! These are the things I remember!"

It went on a while longer, but there really wasn't a resolution. There never is when Americans chew over the Nam War. The North Vietnamese are the only ones who can see it clearly, their images all crystal-clear in the bright wash of victory. For our part, Teddy, the other guy and I were just three guys arguing about our wars. War marks, it defines the survivors for the rest of their lives. Teddy gave up his physical well-being for his war, and I gave up my innocence for mine. And I suppose that, in the aftermath, we each clung to what got us through. For Teddy it was discipline and iron will. For me, it was imagination and risk-taking. No wonder we didn't see eye to eye.

The conversation finally drifted on to other things, and I was grateful for that. It was our last session, and Teddy did a review and a wrap-up of the class accomplishments. I looked at the wall over his head, letting his voice drone on. In some ways, the experience had been worth the effort, but I was glad it was over. It was time to move on.

Once you've got that Top Secret security clearance, sometimes you acquire a taste for spying. Army Security Agency personnel have been known to cross over into the CIA, and even those who don't occasionally get caught up in matters that may be described as more personal and physical than electronic.

TODAY BANANAS

By Hal Castle

It was the baby carriage that caught my eye first. Nothing unusual about women pushing baby carriages in cities, large or small. An ordinary sight, you see it all the time.

But this was no ordinary city and this was no ordinary baby carriage. This was East Berlin in 1987, long before The Wall came down or before the border guards had stopped killing their fellow German Democratic Republic citizens for no longer wanting to live under the rule of the Soviet Union's surrogates in what they called *the worker's paradise.*

The buggy looked like it had come from one of the upper middle class department stores in West Germany, perhaps Kaufhaus or KaDeWe. The wheels had fat rubber tires. There were lots of bright metal levers and adjustment knobs. The bassinet part was in a suspension system that absorbed all the shocks and kept the rider in comfort. It wasn't at all like the ordinary East Berlin buggy, with axles stuck through coiled strips of rusty metal and wheels with thin solid rubber tires and the platform bolded directly to the axles with U-bolts.

I didn't look up as they passed, the baby and the woman, so I noticed her shoes as well. They were flats, but not the flats worn by most women in East Berlin—the ones with cardboard soles and the uppers slued and stretched out of shape to hold the thick woolen socks the ordinary women wore. No, these shoes also looked like they had come from a source in the West, as did the stockings even though they had a run near the heel, painted over with clear nail polish.

After they passed, I looked up at her. Her clothes were not really out of the ordinary, but you could see that they were just a little better than the ones available at the state-owned Kaufhalle where most East Berliners bought their clothes. There was just a tad more sharpness to the pleats and the quality of the material looked better. Her hair, the Roan color of the Selesian ethnic Germans of the Balkan regions, was well cut, and from my view she was pleasant to watch walk. Perhaps she was the mistress of someone high up, or a maid who worked for someone high up, I thought.

I was sitting on a bench across the street from a small, bleak-looking store with a sign in the window, a sign I hadn't seen in that shop before. The sign, hand-written on a piece of pressed board, said in German, "Today Bananas", followed by a high Ost Mark price "per item". The woman went in and returned a short time later with three of the blackest and most over-ripe bananas I had ever seen.

She crossed the street and sat at my bench. She squeezed a bit of the fruit out of the skin of one of the bananas and mixed it between her thumb and finger. She uncovered the child in the buggy and fed the mashed banana to it. She did this over and over until half the fruit was gone.

From the way she looked at, talked and tended to the child, I knew she was the mother. Her hazel eyes had the kind of glisten and light that only a parent displays when tending a precious child. And I suspected that she was the mistress or a former mistress of a high-up party, police or STASI official. There was no way she could have access to the baby buggy, shoes or clothing in East Berlin, but there were ways for influential people to have and enjoy the goods of the West. Still, she couldn't be a wife, because the wife of one of those influentials would not be visiting a grubby produce store on the wrong side of Alexander Platz to buy rotted bananas. The wife would have bought them in one of the special stores reserved for the DDR Nomenklatura. And medicines that the normal East German could only dream about would have been provided at some special state clinic.

"The child is ill?", I asked, speaking in German.

"It's the heart," she nodded. "The doctors say that if she survives for a few years the condition will pass. Hani is two years now and was born ill. Her color is not so good when she cannot have bananas." She explained that the bananas, rotten as they were, were still a source of potassium that just might keep her child alive. The child, Hani, had a bluish tinge to her pale skin and looked too weak to stand, which would explain why she was in a baby buggy long after most would have been being chased by their mother. A mother, desperate for her child, talking to a total stranger on a park bench. I made a mental note.

I was in East Berlin that day, having been given "the right" as a member of the Occupation Forces. I was a retired Senior NCO and the dependent of an active duty Senior NCO. The East Germans didn't like it, but they couldn't keep me out unless I committed a serious crime, something like theft or murder. The Soviets couldn't keep me out either, and they liked my presence even less. They could only keep me from roaming outside the limits of the Soviet Sector that had been set by the four countries that had occupied Berlin since the end of World War II.

My reasons for being in East Berlin were somewhat complicated. I had applied for several jobs with the US forces in West Berlin and a company in the US was looking my resume over, trying to find a match for my skills that they could use in Europe. Just to keep busy, I took a job with the Army PX in West Berlin. I wound up as the manager of the PX loading and receiving dock. I went in cold, but learned the rudiments of the PX job very fast. It doesn't take a rocket scientist to watch three people unload a semi full of products and check them off an inventory sheet while they did it. And you don't have to be Dale Earnhart to drive a forklift.

After a time, probably because of my training in the Army, I noticed a person I felt could use some scrutiny. This fellow constantly went against established PX procedures for returning damaged goods to West

Germany. These items would lie around on a shelf for a while instead of being shipped immediately on the next empty trailer leaving the dock, with the paperwork given to the driver of the tractor. I didn't say anything, but I started to keep an eye on him. I noticed he tended to drive our small van to a particular motor pool where he delivered the broken video recorders and other items. This motor pool was used to park the vehicles of a major Army unit in West Berlin, a unit involved in intelligence activities. And he was very friendly with a Turkish shuttle bus driver employed by the major unit's Logistics shop. I reported my suspicions to a Counterintelligence officer I knew well and told him what I had found out. I also told him that he was inordinately inquisitive about my prior service, where I lived, what my wife did in her job as an active duty Army Non-Commissioned Officer. I gave him the persons name and what I knew about him from a personal standpoint. Within a very short time—less than a week, the person was gone. Vanished. Didn't even collect his last paycheck. At the time I had no idea the bus driver would be implicated in a major espionage effort involving an Officer of the unit. I often wondered about the former PX employee, but nothing I did in the future allowed me to find out.

Eventually the Army got around to telling me that the jobs I had applied for had been filled—there was a regulation that kept any retiree in West Berlin from being hired during the first year out of service, and the company in the States had fit me with a Physical Security Enhancement Program position, within the US's efforts at preventing terrorist attacks on US installations in Europe. I was to liaison with various intelligence and security personnel and prioritize the efforts in each community. This got me introduced to a couple of folks who worked for some of the alphabet agencies, and they asked me if I would become a presence in East Berlin for them, my regular job duties permitting. I agreed and that was how I wound up on the bench, across from a scruffy looking store with a sign saying Today Bananas.

I drove my vehicle, a Ford Aerostar van, here and there around East Berlin. I visited every corner of the city open to Americans, stopping by the various stores and restaurants operated by the Warsaw Pact countries. I established a routine and did my best to become a boring person to follow. My job was to observe and report. My instructions were simple: Don't do anything stupid. Don't become involved. Don't interfere with anything you see.

My days were filled with things to do. I drove the spouses and significant others of visiting VIP's on shopping trips to the stores and outlets that existed for the sole purpose of attracting western currency. I shopped for things that matched my interest in fishing and sailing. I took groups of my neighbor's spouses on similar shopping trips. Sometimes I would drive over for lunch at the Moskva, the Sofia or the Bucharesti.

I made a show of buying Cuban brandy, rum and cigars and bemoaning that we couldn't buy these luxuries back home. Sometimes I would buy specific items that I'd been directed to purchase by the people back in West Berlin; I'd stop in at the Russian store on Karl Marx Platz to buy an all-band radio receiver made in Russia and sold for a paltry 600 East Marks ($60 U.S.), or to buy something else from an East German shop, or the Czech shop.

And sometimes, when the rush and madness of West Berlin just overwhelmed me, I went East for some quiet. Comparing West and East Berlin in 1987 would be like comparing a prima ballerina performing in Swan Lake to a doped up, glassy-eyed pole dancer at Fast Eddie's Grope & Hope Club.

West Berlin was a unique place at that time. Not part of any country, it was it's own political entity, an international city and an island of freedom set in the middle of one of the most repressive countries there was–the Peoples Democratic Republic of East Germany, and The Workers Paradise. There was no direct influence from West Germany allowed, even though the West German Parliament appropriated funds for the city. No

West German soldiers were permitted into the city, and the citizens of West Berlin were not subject to any of the laws of West Germany unless they traveled to the West. Many of the young men in the universities and colleges of West Berlin were legal draft evaders, since Berliners could not be drafted in the West German military.

West Berlin was bustling, thriving, almost throbbing. Traffic was constant, even in the middle of the Gruenewald around Teuffelsberg, Devils Mountain, built from World War II rubble. There were very few quiet places. The city was full of people who knew what was across the wall; they seemed hell-bent on enjoying their good life, aware that if their karma went wrong, they might similarly become prisoners of the sick and defeating system that existed on the other side of the wall. Like scenes repeating themselves from Cabaret, there was gaiety both forced and real.

On the other hand, the traffic in East Berlin was very light, with the occasional Trabant or two-stroke gas-oil burning Wartburg putting and smoking down the overly wide boulevards and streets. I wasn't lulled; I saw the streets as wide passageways for the machines of war to travel westward if the order ever came to move into West Berlin. It was a little odd by Western standards; there were more military vehicles, police vehicles and official vehicles than private ones. Convoys of Russians scurried everywhere, their diesel motors growling and spewing black smoke. And one could pick out the conspicuous cars of the elite, the Mercedes with private DDR plates that were driven by well-fed, well-groomed men and women. There was an occasional Porsche, Volvo or Saab, as well as VW Golf sedans and Jettas.

East Berlin was grim, with only an occasional smiling face to be seen, usually in a park where some doting parent was watching a child innocently playing, unaware of its surroundings. Most of the people went quietly about their business. As they went, they might glance surreptitiously at the cars and the clothing of the well dressed and usually over-fed Westerners. There may have been places from which love and warmth, music and laughter spilled freely, places where the mood was not a forced pretense to convince the foreigners that all was great in *the worker's paradise.* But if such places existed, I never found them.

There were STASI vehicles escorting Russian officers in khaki-colored Lada Sedans. In '86, an East Berliner had acquired three Russian uniforms, that of a private and two officers. Then he painted a Hungarian car to look like a Lada. Using cleverly forged documents, he had gotten past the East German border guards at Checkpoint Charlie, and escaped to West Berlin. It was not an unusual attempt at attaining freedom, the citizens of East Berlin tried constantly to flee the repression and soul deadening Communist state. Many died in their attempts, shot by their fellow citizens or mauled to death by the Doberman Pincer dogs trained to apprehend those fleeing between the cruel rows of steel wire fencing, topped with razor wire.

It was one of the normal STASI escort trips that persuaded me to break my orders and become involved.

By this time, I included in my routine the habit of loitering near the shop where the "Today Bananas" sign had been, to check on the young mother and little baby Hani. I figured there had to be a tremendously active grapevine of underground information, because she never appeared unless the sign was up. I would sit on the bench across the street, eating a simple German lunch, an open-faced wurst sandwich, a snap-top beer and some fruit. I would bring bananas if I could find any at the commissary.

On this day, the woman with the baby carriage was waiting in line with about a half dozen people in front of her when a Russian military sedan pulled up, accompanied by the STASI escort. The Russian talked the East German official and then pointed to the bananas in the shop. The STASI officer pointed to the people in the line, and the STASI guy pointed to the khaki Lada with the red star on the door. To me they both looked unhappy, but seemed resigned to the situation. The fruit vender held up five fingers of one hand.

The STASI officer nodded, and the man put one "hand" of bananas under the counter. The Russians were invited in, and quickly purchased all the bananas on top of the display case. The vendor and the STASI East German officer were not pleased, but there was nothing they could do. The Russians were the masters, and they would have their way, no matter what the East Germans wanted or needed.

The Russian directed the STASI officer to pay for the bananas. He didn't look happy, but he did as he was told. After they left, the line started up again. He sold one banana to each customer, but the supply was gone before the young mother and her child got there. The "Today Bananas" sign came down. She and the others looked crestfallen, and maybe a little desperate. Who knows? Maybe there were plans for a special desert, for a birthday or some other celebration. I did know there was one woman with a need for potassium to keep her little girl alive.

I watched her push the baby buggy across the street. As before, she sat on the bench beside me. She cooed at her child, and sighed deeply. To me, it seemed there was some improvement in the child's color and alertness. Would this current setback cause a medical setback? It seemed clear to me that fate or chance had spoken to me. I had a banana, left over from my lunch, wrapped in tissue in the pocket of my greatcoat.

I slid it quietly across the distance on the bench between us.

"For the child," I said.

She saw instantly what it was. She took it, slipping it swiftly into her coat pocket, even as her face revealed she could scarcely believe her luck.

"Danke," She said. "Danke. Danke."

That was how it started. I had, of course, broken one of the cardinal rules. I had become involved. At least, I told myself, I was simply trying to help out a sick kid with little or no prospect for a healthy future. I didn't see it as much of a transgression; after all, I'd been involved with sick and orphaned kids in Vietnam, Laos, Thailand, Okinawa, D'Jibouti and The Affars…places all over the world where I'd been in the service of the Army Security Agency. I didn't stop to think through what the larger consequences might be for the child, the mother, or me. For me, back then, helping the kid was enough.

The East Germans probably couldn't have done anything to me. Surveillance had slacked off over the months since I'd been pulling my routine, and I was only occasionally followed from Checkpoint Charlie to my first sitting bench, store or restaurant. I had a boring routine, and I followed it religiously, and so was very low on the radar screen of the East German Watchers. Had we been caught, had any watcher noticed and reported that simple exchange, the consequences for the woman could have been severe. But we weren't thinking about that.

From then on, I made it a point to carry bananas with me each time I went to the other side of The Wall. If there was an opportunity to give them to her, I did. Occasionally, when she didn't show up, I was tempted to give them to some other East German who might need them, but I never did. The risk was too great. I didn't need the attention. And so I went about, bringing bananas to a person I hardly knew while 1987 faded into a cold, gray winter that gradually became the blustery and wet spring.

It was in February or March of 1988 when she asked if I was an American.

"Yes," I replied. "How did you know that, Fraulein?"

"Please, call me Silvie. After your help we should not be formal. I've seen your mini-bus when you park near the Sporthalle, in the square between the apartment buildings."

"Do you live near there?" I was suddenly sweating bullets. I had no training on how to interview East Germans, no brief on how to have this sort of conversation with anyone who had figured out that I was an American. It was different from chatting with an East Berlin policeman trying to move me along, say, a policeman reluctant to call a Russian to deal with me.

"In the vicinity, yes" Silvie replied. "Not far, in fact."

"Nice area. Quiet. Not much traffic." I tried to look matter-of-fact.

"Yes. And my little girl rests well in the quiet." She paused, looking down at her hands; "I want to thank you for your kindness."

"Hani is better. That is enough thanks."

"So, what is America like? Is it as poor as we have been told?"

I smiled. "No. America is not poor. We have as many fresh bananas as we want, and they only cost pennies. And we have no Wall."

I was afraid I would exhaust my limited German, or we would be noticed. I got up and bid her Good Day. When I got back to the west side of the Wall, I called my contact and arranged a meeting.

We met at the Gasthaus Alte Steinkrug, deep inside the American Zone not far from the U.S. Army hospital. He didn't seem unhappy. "So," he said, "you had a conversation with a single mother with a sick bid. That's not bad. The surveillance is off you now, you know."

I nodded and took a sip from my cold glass of Berliner Kindl, "I figured it was." I glanced over at the old Burger who seemed to always be in the place. The staff catered to his every whim, calling him Herr Doktor. He carried a thermometer specially made to check the temperature of the seemingly endless steins of draft beer they brought him. Unlike my contact, who dressed as a European but was in good shape, the old man had jowls and gray hair jutting in all directions from under his fisherman style hat. His complexion was ruddy, with spider-webs of tiny blood vessels on his cheeks. I suspected his eyes were rheumy behind his glasses. "They almost never follow you past the Meisen Porcelain shop, and never past Alexander Platz."

I wiped the watery rings from the table with the palm of my hand, "What should I do?"

"Keep up your normal routine, and keep taking bananas with you. Let's see what happens."

So through the summer of 1988, I took bananas with me across the border. We met on the familiar park bench and I had fleeting conversations with young Silvie. Her apartment overlooked the place where I often parked my van. We talked about her baby daughter, Hani. I tried to satisfy her curiosity about "the West."

Then, in July, she told me she had something to give me. I could see by the look in her eyes it was something I might have to be careful about. I told her to wait a few days. "Meet me in the Kaufhalle, children's section, on Friday at about 2 in the afternoon. Don't worry."

Easy for me to say. But the truth is, I was plenty worried. After all, she was an unknown factor, and I was a rank novice with minimal training and very little tradecraft in the arena of Soviet influence. In the past, when I had come up with an idea the people in the Berlin U.S. command approved it. I was simply a "cut-out", a front for the people in the East to use to get information from or to West Berlin. I would try to keep it simple.

When we met that Friday, told her to put whatever she had inside the gas flap of a bright yellow Mercedes that I was driving. I told her where it was parked, and we went separate ways. When I got back to the yellow 280 SEL, the gas flap was tightly closed. I was tempted to take a peek inside, but drove instead to West Berlin and the Alte Steinkrug.

After picking up my contact, we drove to the closest BP service station. I drove up to a gas pump, and my passenger got out to fill the tank. I triggered the cover flap from the inside and he took whatever was there and pumped in a few liters of gas. I remember he paid with the PX sold gas coupons we all used. I took him back to his car at the beer hall. "I'll be in touch," he said as he drove away.

A few days later he called. "Let's meet at the Berlin American Yacht Club." The yacht club was over on the Wannsee portion of the river that ran through West Berlin. When I arrived, he'd already rigged a J-20 for a sail. We went out on the water and sailed toward the British Zone, where they had their own sailing club.

"About that stuff you brought out?" he said. "It has some importance."

"Well, I'm glad I didn't buy all those bananas for nothing."

"You would have bought them anyway."

"True…"

He squinted in the direction of the sun, which seemed about to be swallowed by some afternoon clouds. It wasn't really a pleasant day for sailing, and we were almost alone on the river. "You have to come up with a way to take information to her. A secure way."

"How about inside the bananas?" I'd been sharing my fruit with her for months, and she always put it in her pocket or bag. She usually went home before giving any to her baby, Hani.

"Could work, I guess…" He thought about it for a few minutes while we sailed.

"Yes," he finally decided, "It will work very well, in fact. We don't have to worry about finding a good drop, or wasting resources watching the drop. You use the banana and she uses the gas flap." By this time we were at the British club, so we decided to dock and have lunch. We pulled up to a tie-off buoy and I did a respectable jibe to position the boat to where he could grab it with a hook. A motorboat came out and took us onboard.

"Does your friend like British beer then?" the boatman asked my contact.

"Anything better than Berliner Kindl would be great. We sat at a table and I drank Newcastle Brown Ale. We had a British London Grill Lunch. Unremarkable for the English, who have a knack bringing their homeland along with them, no matter where they go. I walked out on a dock while my contact talked with his friend. Lunch over, the Brit took us back out to our J-20. I took the tiller and my contact ran the sheets and sails.

A couple days later he called and requested we meet at the beer hall. When I arrived, he threw a briefcase in the back seat of the Aerostar and directed me to drive over through the Green Forest toward Teufelsberg, where a major intelligence US Army site was located.

"I think I have just what you need, my friend," he said.

I had to drive up the artificial hill and into the site's compound before he would open his briefcase.

"Do you people always act so paranoid?" I kidded. "Why didn't you just come over to my house?"

He smiled sadly and shook his head. "Wish I could, but they watch us here much harder than we ever can over on their side. We have to be far more careful…you wouldn't want your friend compromised, would you?"

No surprise…inside his case were a couple of bananas. At least that's what they looked like at first glance. He picked one up and showed me where it was split down the side of one of the inside curves. It was plastic, but it looked enough like a slightly over-ripe banana to fool me. It even felt like a banana. Maybe a little lighter, but the same feel. He pulled the split apart and took out a few sheets of rolled-up notepaper.

"Invisible ink?" I asked.

"Blanks," he grinned. "this is just the demonstration for the mule…"

"Ohh…" I understood he was talking about me. I wasn't on a *need to know* basis.

"Best you never read anything you carry either way across the Wall."

"I was kind of curious to see what she gave me that first time."

"And did you look?"

"No, and I'm glad I didn't. This kind of work is getting a little too deep for my liking. I'm more of an electronic covert type. I like things like hearing Dit Dah and knowing it means Alpha…home row, little finger."

"You don't want to back out, do you?" He was giving me my one and only chance.

"No, of course not."

"Good. From now on, this is your only project. Continue to go over as often as you can, but your only real purpose will be to service this asset." He was, of course, talking about the young mother. The spy business can be cold as ice about people and their fate. He continued, "We know you're not trained. Truth is, sometimes that can make you better at what we need you to do."

"Ignorance is bliss?"

"No, something else. You won't get lazy and comfortable. I don't think you'll make mistakes."

Since the "Today Bananas" sign generally appeared in the shop between Tuesday and Thursday, we decided that I was to go over all three days if needed.

"Do we have a back-up plan? Maybe some other place I might meet her?" I asked.

"I don't think so. That could be dangerous for both of you. You meet her mid-week, like always, and then do a pick-up on Friday if she has anything for us."

And so it went for the rest of the summer and into the fall. I made several deliveries of real and plastic bananas, and left the gas flap open on the Mercedes for her drop-offs. One day in October my contact called and asked if we could meet at the Burger King on the American PX compound. As I arrived, he got in my car and told me to drive over towards the Ku Damm (Kurfursten Damm Strasse).

"Your instructions," he said, "are to be at the Reichstag, at the main entrance on Wednesday at about 1500, hang around for an hour or so. Let me out over there." That was all he said. I pulled over and he got out without saying another word.

I arrived a little early at the Reichtag. I wandered around, doing tourist things. When the time came, I made sure I was outside at the main entrance, looking out over the Spee River. From where I was, I could see the Wall on the other side, curving away to the north. At this point, part of the East Berlin U-Banh rail transport system ran on a bridge that arched over the Spee River. As I watched, a train came to a halt on the bridge that arched over the Spee. Three people got off the train. There were two men and women. They paused, and then suddenly all three of them dove into the river and swam as hard as they could for the bank on the West Berlin side.

I didn't think they had a chance, because an East German border patrol boat appeared from around the bend. I knew those boats. They were diesel powered and very fast. The engines roared to high speed and the boat headed directly towards the swimmers. I could see one of the crewmen, looking like a tiny doll in the distance, as he jumped to the forward 12.75mm machinegun. Then I noticed a group of men on the west bank, about 50 yards from the Bundestag. They were running down to the water's edge while another man with a shoulder-held video camera taped the scene. When the crew on the boat saw the video camera, they motioned the gunner not to fire. The gun barrel dropped and the boat sped on past the swimmers, disappearing around the bend, heading back to East Berlin.

The swimmers were pulled from the water and whisked off in several big Mercedes vans. The man with the video camera turned in my direction. I thought he looked very much like the Brit I'd met at the yacht club. He gave me an open-palmed salute. *British to the core,* I thought, smiling to myself. The show was obviously over, and I turned and went on my way. That evening all the television stations in West Berlin stations, except the French Army one, ran the tape the Brit had made.

My contact called a few days later. We met in the lobby of the American Hospital and sat in the hospital mess hall. He eyed me over his cup of lousy coffee.

"Take one more run for us," he said. "Tell her all is well. *Alles gut.*"

"And *danka?*"

"And thanks," he smiled.

"What now? What about me?"

"Your pass to East Berlin is being pulled. You've no need to go there any more." His slow smile crept across the lines of his face, "After all, you've bought at least one of everything there is to buy over there."

I nodded, "Too dangerous…"

His smile broadened, "we can get someone else to go to the Meisen Shop, if we need that. You've done well for us. Very well."

"What about the kid? What about the bananas? The kid needs potassium or she'll die."

He shifted uneasily, "I don't know. We haven't forgotten about the child. We just don't know what to do.

I thought I might have an idea. "What's the clearance level of the Hospital Commander here? He must have a Top Secret at least. He's a Colonel, right?"

"Whoa, don't go so fast. You mean Colonel Blanck?"

"Right. Commander at this hospital, where we are drinking rotten coffee at this minute."

"He's pretty well connected, as a matter of fact…why do you ask?"

"Because he can give me a two year supply of potassium for a little girl with a bad heart. And you can get me the bananas to take it over in."

"Hmmm. Might work. But let's not bother the Colonel. I'll handle it.

"Throw in some multi-vitamins for the mother. She's been looking a little ragged lately."

"All right, softy," he sighed.

"It's what you get when you deal with amateurs," I smiled.

I got the pills two days later. I never knew how my contact procured them, but the markings seemed to indicate that they were Hungarian. They fit in five bananas, along with instructions for taking the pills.

"Why not more?" I asked.

"Greedy, greedy," he said. "Don't worry, my friend. These are very concentrated. They will be more than enough."

I went back over to East Berlin and sat on the bench across from the shop. Tuesday, Wednesday, and Thursday there was no "Today Bananas" sign, no mother, and no child.

On Saturday, a voice I didn't recognize called on my home phone. "The sign is up," the muffled voice said. It felt a little strange to me; I drove over to Checkpoint Charlie with feelings of misgivings. My contact was waiting in the MP shack when I went in to sign the crossing roster. He nodded to me and pointed to the parking lot.

"I got this call. I didn't know who it was. I'm a little nervous…"

"No. It's a valid call. Go ahead. Good luck."

"And let me add my wishes while I congratulate you on a very fine job." said a voice in the accent the Southern Appalachians. I turned and there stood the old Burger from the Alte Stein Krug, hair still straying in all directions, but with clear eyes and clearer skin.

"He's our Control, he watches out for all of us and makes things happen when we need them to get done," my contact told me.

He could have felled me with a limp, wet beer mat.

I got in my Aerostar. It was busy that day, and getting across the East Berlin border patrol checkpoint seemed to take forever. There was only one lane into and out of East Berlin. The guards were stopping all the cars. They wouldn't let us pass while they conducted a minute examination of the car in front of us, a beat-up Fiat with Polish license plates. A man was driving the Fiat. He had a woman passenger and two kids in the back seat. The East Germans were looking at the seals and stamps and marks on his passport with a magnifying glass. They were trying to find some reason to turn them back from West Berlin. After nearly an hour, they still had found nothing and so had to allow them to cross into the East. I saw the expression on the woman's face turn from tearful fright to pure bliss. Good for her, but I had my own problems.

By this time I was desperate to get to the shop. I was almost sure I would miss the mother and her kid. When I got there, she wasn't anywhere in sight. Had I missed her? I tried to calm myself. It had been less than three hours since I received the phone call. I parked in a lot on the opposite side of the street from the store and just happened to look in the direction of the Sporthalle. I couldn't be sure, but a couple of blocks away there was a woman pushing a baby carriage. It could be here. She was going towards the apartment square where I parked when she made her drop-offs.

I drove down the street, and it was her! And I immediately did the dumbest thing in my brief career as an amateur spy. I did a U-turn right in front of two East German civil police cars headed in the opposite direction. That time, the fates smiled on me. The police simply honked and waved their fists, yelling at me, "Stupid!" And then they sped off into the distance.

She looked shocked, no doubt thinking I was crazy to make a move like that in front of the German authorities. I slowed the van as I approached her and pointed back towards the "Bananas Today" sign. She nodded and turned her baby carriage around, heading towards the usual bench where we had met so many times before.

When I arrived, she was already sitting.

"So," she said simply.

I handed her the bag with the five plastic bananas.

Her eyes raised, "So much! What do they want, to spend so much?"

"Not bananas. Pills." I split open one of the bananas to show what they contained. "For your little Hani. And for you, Silvie. A two years supply."

"It is a dream come true."

"And they said to tell you *Alles gut.*"

Tears welled in her eyes. "Then this is *Auf weider'sehn?*"

"Yes. I'm going back to America. I won't be back. Take care of your daughter. And take care of yourself. Maybe one day we'll meet again."

We sat there for a few minutes, not holding hands, not even touching. She sighed occasionally, and her well-sculpted bosom heaved.

And then I got back in the Aerostar and drove back across the border. Maybe one day we will meet again. I'd like to know that the kid made it, grew up to be a strong and healthy teenager. And the mother…well, you know, when you're an amateur spy like me, you don't get all crusty and cold. You get to care for people, and what happens to them.

0-595-21729-X